Person and Persona

Person and Persona

Studies in Shakespeare
by
Gwyn Williams

CARDIFF
UNIVERSITY OF WALES PRESS
1981

British Library Cataloguing in Publication Data

Williams, Gwyn
    Person and persona.
    I. Title
    822.3'3   PR 2976

    ISBN 0-7083-0784-1

Typesetting by Afal, Cardiff
Printed by South Western Printers Ltd., Caerphilly

To Frank Owen

*whose Westham House enabled me
to develop the ideas in this book.*

Contents

Preface

These essays are the product of a lifetime of studying and lecturing on Shakespeare, pulled together, that is my hope, by the Introduction. 'Black Beauty in Shakespeare' has appeared in earlier forms in *Personal Landscape* (London, 1945) and *Bulletin of Studies* (Benghazi, 1959); 'Sea-storm, Tide Imagery and Mutiny in Shakespeare' in *Litera* (Istanbul, 1965); *'The Comedy of Errors* Rescued from Tragedy' in *A Review of English Literature* (London, 1964); 'Suffolk and Margaret' in *Shakespeare Quarterly* (*S.Q.* 25 (1974), 310-322, Washington.); 'Welshmen in Shakespeare's Stratford' and *'Troelus a Chresyd:* a Welsh Tragedy' in *Transactions of the Honourable Society of Cymmrodorion* (London, 1955 and 1958). I wish to thank the editors of the above-mentioned book and periodicals for permission to republish them here. The Introduction, 'Seals of Love', *'The Taming of the Shrew'* and 'The Loneliness of the Homosexual' are new and not previously published.

My gratitude is also due to Mr John Rhys, Director of the University of Wales Press, for his encouraging interest in this book and his ready and unfailing helpfulness in its preparation, to a reader who saved me from a wrong attribution and to the staff of the Press for their meticulous work. G.W.

Introduction

Much has been written during the past two hundred years about the "characters" of Shakespeare, and the persons of his plays, the *dramatis personae*, have been considered as though they had a life of their own, could exist outside the play, with a life before the play begins and after the play ends. This is a practice which L. C. Knights wittily satirised in his essay, *How Many Children Had Lady Macbeth?* Such criticism has produced much fine writing and has enabled critic after critic to express his personality and to adumbrate the ideals and concerns of his age and of the community to which he belongs. So there is much interesting reading to be found along the road from Maurice Morgann to Jan Kott. But such criticism, though serving some pleasant and useful purposes, has taken us away from Shakespeare, for it has usually been forgotten that these persons in his plays are his invention, that they are not people he has created to set loose in the world but that they do not exist outside the plays. They are puppets, amazingly complex puppets it is true, but puppets he has devised so that he may analyse patterns of human behaviour. It is we who are drawn into the plays rather than the "characters" that are set free. It is important therefore to keep it in mind that every person in the plays is an aspect of Shakespeare, a device through which the dramatist offers us his view of the human condition. So, following the phrase *dramatis personae,* I use the words persons, not characters, for these creations.

And why persona? Though Shakespeare was clearly disturbed by the contemporary incidence of melancholy in the late 1590s he shows little interest in or dependence on physical, medical or psychological approaches to the evaluation of the human personality. He would I think find himself closer to modern European attempts to interpret man's behaviour than to the medieval inheritance of ancient systems, and to the Elizabethan fashion of the four humours rather than to the ancient Greek four constituent fluids, of blood, black bile, yellow bile and phlegm. Adam Smith's economic man, driven on by greed; Kretschmer's three types of bodily structure; Freud's id, ego and superego; Adler's stimulant of the drive to power and superiority; all these may be found exemplified in Shakespeare. And he knew of the human tendency, the human need very often, to adopt a persona, as explained by Jung, to project a public image of oneself as one would like to be received. Shakespeare's central study of this urge I find in *The Taming of the Shrew*.

The word persona may originally have been Etruscan and was used for the mask worn by players on the ancient stage of classical drama, a mask whose mouthpiece could have helped the projection of the voice, which established the mood of the play by its smiling or scowling formation and which spared the audience the mouthings and grimaces we now suffer in the theatre, by concentrating on the voice and the words and diminishing the likelihood of the person played by the actor being accepted as a living being. The players were thus accepted as puppets. This word persona was used by Jung for the behavioural mask we try to put between ourselves and the people about us, even in the most intimate of situations, as in the relationship between Katherina and Petruchio. Every one of us to some degree acts a part in order to persuade others to accept us as what we like to think we are, or what we would like to be. The extreme form of this is to try to persuade others that we are Napoleon or Jesus Christ. So the famous speech from *As You Like It,* beginning,

> All the world's a stage
> And all the men and women merely players . . .

does more than record the observation that our lives fall neatly enough into a classification which provides the theatre with stock characters, to use the stock phrase. (It is worth noting here that in Elizabethan English the word *merely* meant *purely, entirely,* without our present-day dismissive sense of *only.*) To me the speech suggests that within and beyond this or some similar classification into which all men fall (women are perhaps not so easy to classify), we all individually act self-chosen parts in order to peg out a claim for attention to our particular identity and personality, sometimes falsifying the real person for reasons of our own. I will note the parts played by the persons in *The Taming of the Shrew* and the reasons for the view of themselves which they contrive to present.

The function of the persona is often to establish a satisfactory relationship with other individuals and with the society of which one is part, and sets of different human relationships provide the pattern of all Shakespeare's plays. His favourite word for a recognised human relationship was *bond*, an old legal term, and sometimes the business term *contract.* If in a play a bond or a set of bonds is tested, is brought under strain but survives, is patched up or develops into a richer association, then the play is usually classed as a comedy. If important bonds are cracked (a favourite word of Shakespeare's for the breakdown of a relationship) and there is nothing to replace them, then the play is usually considered as tragic, especially if a death is involved. These are critics' terms and Shakespeare refused to accept the classical notion of pure comedy and pure tragedy, in spite of the mockery of Ben Jonson and of Sir Philip Sidney's insistence on the following of the three unities of time, place and action. In fact, Shakespeare seems deliberately to have adopted what Sidney, in his *Apologie for Poetrie,* put forward as absurd faults and successfully incorporated them into his plays, especially in *Henry V, The Winter's Tale* and *The Tempest. Hamlet* comes near to complete tragedy, for all the important bonds are broken for Hamlet except that of Horatio's friendship, which comforts his dying moments. And even here the Gravediggers find fun in death. Friendship may for Shakespeare have been the deepest and most necessary bond, whilst that of love is sealed with a kiss, as the document of a contract is sealed with the moulding of red wax, one of the dramatist's most telling images thus springing from his business preoccupations. (In *Sea-storm, Tide Imagery and Mutiny* I have tried to show how a literary experience can tie up with personal observation as a source of imagery.) Important bonds may clash and lead to the painful and often destructive experience of a conflict of loyalties, as when the love of Romeo and Juliet is pitted against solidarity with their feuding families. A classical case is that of Sophocles' Antigone, torn between love of and duty to her brother and her obedience to the state.

   To exemplify such conflicts and to analyse the strain which life puts upon the different human relationships, Shakespeare carefully and deliberately selects the dramatic persons he needs to set a particular problem. So there are plays in which we have poignant parent-child relationships, *Othello, Hamlet, The Comedy of Errors,* and the plays of the last period with their fascinating series of daughters; *Love's Labours Lost* and *Timon of Athens,* where the persons seem to be of one generation; and *Coriolanus,* a play with three generations to help us understand the attitude of Coriolanus towards his country and how he acquired this attitude.

In the process of noting the different bond-patterns which Shakespeare set out to demonstrate and analyse in each of his plays I found myself devising a simple figure which not only helped my awareness of the purpose of each play but allowed me to do some rudimentary self-analysis. I have also applied it to some of my friends and relatives, to Shakespeare himself from what we know of his life and to Dafydd ap Gwilynr, chiefly from the evidence of his poems.

Here is the figure. You take a sheet of paper — a postcard does well — and place a dot in the middle. This is you, or the person in the play, or any living thing, for to himself or herself or itself every living thing is the centre of the universe. From this point you draw lines radiating clockwise to the edges of the card. These lines represent relationships. First, again following a clockwise order, come the involuntary bonds, those into which one is born, without having any say in the matter oneself, parents, grandparents, brothers and sisters, uncles, aunts and cousins. At the bottom of the card come neighbours and they overlap into the next half since, although you are born into a community, it is possible to move out of it and to choose a new neighbourhood. From here upwards to the top of the card come the voluntary relationships. These are children, usually planned or hoped for but sometimes arriving unwanted, and so involuntary. Friends follow, love partners, marriage partners, fellow workers, practitioners of the same craft or profession, fellow members of clubs and societies and political parties. Finally, at the top, comes your country. This is involuntary too, but it is possible to change your nationality. Obviously, a person well endowed along the greatest number of these lines will be the best integrated into his society and is likely to be the happiest. At the same time he has lent the greatest number of hostages to fortune, whilst deficiency along a number of lines may be compensated by a concentration upon a few. It is interesting to observe how Lear, Macbeth and Richard III work out according to this figure and what happens to their different bonds.

The persona is a device for presenting the kind of personality one wishes to be acknowledged as possessing, and I take one's personality to mean the *kind* of person one is. This mask is sometimes allowed to slip and the intention is for the moment revealed. There is a significant moment in *Henry IV Part I,* Act II, sc. iv, a moment which the quick business of the stage does not allow us to take in fully without further consideration. Prince Hal is acting the part of his father, Falstaff that of the prince. As the prince, Falstaff pleads against his banishment from the prince's company. Prince Hal's response is, "I do. I will." That is, "Acting the part of my father, I now banish Falstaff from the prince's company. When I am king I will banish Falstaff from my company." This in fact is what he does when he becomes king, thereby breaking Falstaff's heart. By the end of *Part II* and the beginning of *Henry V* we realise that Hal had all the time been acting a part as a youthful playboy, taking his role in the English myth of the young man who sows his wild oats, to sober up when he comes of age and responsibilities loom. The transformation is not miraculous, as the bishops piously proclaim, but cold-blooded and deliberate. I have never known an actor fully convey this complexity of persona.

If your personality is the kind of person you are, then your identity is who and what you are. This too needs recognition and acceptance on the part of those about you. If no one recognises you as a poet then you are not a poet, and refusal on the part of others to recognise you as what you think you are can lead to despair and madness. The unpleasantness of such a situation is the main theme of *The Comedy of Errors*; it brings anxious moments to *The Taming of the Shrew* and *Twelfth Night*. This has become a theme of modern fiction, as in *Cards of Identity* by Nigel Dennis and *Where No Wounds Were* by Goronwy Rees.

Plays of English history were in vogue when Shakespeare began to write for the theatre and one way to establish himself was to give the public such plays, but though there is plenty of evidence that he studied the chronicles carefully, it is clear that he handled the material he got from them in the most free fashion, seizing upon mere hints to write the kind of scene which interested him and using such inventions to tackle the problems of his own war-weary age. So *Henry IV* and *Henry V* became studies of the aristocratic pursuit of honour and of the relative merits of peace and war. In *Henry IV* Falstaff declines the grinning honour of death, whilst in *Henry V* the speech of the soldier Williams about the awful responsibility for the declaration of war is counterbalanced by Burgundy's splendid speech about the beauties of peace. It is tempting to read Shakespeare's own boredom with straight history into Henry's impatience with the Archbishop of Canterbury's long-drawn-out and incomprehensible application of the Salic Law to Henry's claim to parts of France.

Shakespeare uses a chronicle as freely as he does an Italian novella. In *Henry VI*, his very first use of English history, Shakespeare expands a hint of affection between the Duke of Suffolk and Queen Margaret into a horrifying and unhistorical play within a play, a first study on his part of destructive love, altogether daring behaviour on the part of a dramatist attempting to break into the closed circle of university wits.

It was this same freedom which enabled Shakespeare to demonstrate his interest in Welshness, notably in the persons of Glendower, Captain Fluellen and the schoolmaster Sir Hugh Evans. Shakespeare's view and treatment of Glendower is far fuller and more sympathetic than that of Holinshed and he gives us delightful inventions such as the courtship of Owen's daughter by the captive Mortimer. This same scene poses an intriguing question which may some day be answered, in Glendower's proud response to the mockery of Hotspur.

> I can speak English, Lord, as well as you,
> For I was train'd up in the English court,
> Where being but young I framed to the harp
> Many an English ditty lovely well,
> And gave that tongue a helpful ornament.

We know that Glyndŵr spent some years studying law at the Inns of Court, but no verse by him has yet come to light. Is it possible that Shakespeare could have come upon such verses, and poems by the Duke of Suffolk too, in the library of the Earl of Southampton, to which he would have had access? If this is so, then Glyndŵr may have been the first Welshman to write poetry in English, preceding Ieuan ap Hywel Swrdwal, who in any case really wrote Welsh verse in English which is spelt as Welsh. Or was this view of Owain Glyndŵr inspired by Thomas Jenkins, who became schoolmaster at Stratford when Shakespeare was eleven, for whom Glyndŵr may well have been a hero and who may have provided the dramatist with his material for Sir Hugh Evans?

In Captain Fluellen there is surely a good deal of Sir Roger Williams, one of Elizabeth's most experienced and dependable generals, trusted by her to curb the exuberance of the young noblemen for whom war was a game and a path to personal honour. Sir Roger had written books on the theory and practice of war and Shakespeare would certainly know about him, even if he had not met him at the houses of Southampton or Essex. Fluellen is equally keen on the disciplines of war but although the name Fluellen, an anglicised form of Llywelyn, occurred in Stratford in Shakespeare's day, the strategy and tactics of warfare were not subjects the young dramatist would hear discussed in his native town. These links with

Welshmen resident in Shakespeare's Stratford tempted me to spend a week at the Birthplace Library there, noting everything I could about its Welsh men and women in Shakespeare's day. One of the following essays is a report upon that week's work.

We do not know who wrote the Welsh tragedy of *Troelus a Chresyd* and until we do we can make no conjecture of a possible meeting with Shakespeare, but I have included a study of this play because it carries a story also used by Shakespeare, and because the story is treated so very differently in the two plays. For the Welsh author Troelus's love is in the *cavaliere servente* tradition, Pandar is a good friend, there is no viperish Thersites, but the story is carried through to poor Cresyd's pitiful death as a begging leper at the gate of Troy. For Shakespeare the tale gave the opportunity to work off several kinds of disgust. There had been much interest in different versions of the Trojan War, in poetry, drama and translation, but Shakespeare killed this as a source of material for drama. Then through Thersites, who is in Homer but not in Chaucer or Henryson, he makes bitter mockery of love and war, the fickleness of love and the absurd causes and beastly conduct of war. Shakespeare's play is one of the sharpest and occasionally the most scurrilous attacks on humanity ever made, whereas the Welsh dramatist clings to vestiges of the more sympathetic psychology of Chaucer and Henryson.

So many Welshmen had followed the Tudors to London and prospered there that they were not generally much liked, though from the evidence of the drama of the day they do not seem to have been so disliked as were the Scots, the Irish and the Jews. Elizabethan and Jacobean drama has many comic and satirical treatments of Welshmen (well put together in Dr J.O. Bartley's *Teague, Shenkin and Sawney*) and many jokes about their use of English and the peculiarities of their attitude to life. Shakespeare, with his considerable acquaintance with Welsh people in Stratford and London, is one of the kindest in all this and I like to think that this is in line with a readiness on his part to sympathise with a disliked minority, represented in his plays by such persons as Shylock, Glendower, Aaron, Othello and the two Antonios, of *The Merchant of Venice* and *Twelfth Night*. Shakespeare's unfashionable sympathy with black or swarthy skin is prominent in at least four of his plays, he was the first dramatist to make a black man a tragic hero, and the number of love affairs, courtships and marriages between black men and white women in his plays is quite exceptional. The source of this interest and sympathy may actually have been a black woman, Lucy Negro, an entertainer who took part in a show put on by the Earl of Southampton, Shakespeare's friend and patron, in 1594, and who may be the black woman of *The Sonnets*, for from the evidence of the poems it is wrong to pass her off as simply ''dark''.

The last of my disliked minorities, in Shakespeare's society and to varying degrees in ours, is that of homosexuals, male and female. The plays give us the two Antonios I have already mentioned and Emilia, in Shakespeare's part of *The Two Noble Kinsmen*. To me there is no doubt about the interest of both Antonios in Sebastian and Bassanio respectively (is there some clue in the similarity of the names?) and Emilia is explicit in talking about her experience of love. Shakespeare chiefly sympathises with these persons in their silent apartness at the end of the plays, when other people are celebrating heterosexual love unions. The *Sonnets* too have been thought to express a closeness at least on the poet's own part to a homosexual experience.

In creating these dramatic persons and in revealing their occasional use of the persona, Shakespeare not only illuminated problems and anxieties for his own age but continues to do this for us too. It is for such light, as well as for the poetry, the humour and the pathos, that I re-read the plays and poems and sometimes go to the theatre in the hope that the production will reflect this illumination.

Seals of Love

It seems quite normal today, and not particularly poetical, to say that we seal a promise, a pledge, an engagement or a marriage with a kiss. I remember dancing to a tune called *In a Little Spanish Town* and singing the words,

> We made a promise and sealed it with a kiss.

It was Shakespeare who invented this metaphor, as he did many others that are in common use as part of the English language today. Before him letters had been sealed to keep their contents secret and sealed lips were said to keep secrets too. But no one had thought of lips sealing a contract between lovers, of a kiss being the equivalent of the red wax on the parchment of a legal document. It is even possible to suggest the very moment when the image occurred to the dramatist. Shakespeare was a business man as well as a poet and dramatist and as he wrote there must sometimes have been contracts in preparation or already sealed contracts on his table, almost alongside the manuscript of a play or a poem. Juliet is lying, seemingly dead, in a tomb and the desperate Romeo is about to kill himself. Shakespeare has here to project himself and to see Juliet through the eyes of his creation, Romeo, but he is still the man who may have signed a contract half an hour before. Through Romeo he attempts several striking images to explain the continuing lifelike appearance of Juliet's face, until the final extraordinary image comes, in the words,

> . . . . lips, O you,
> The doors of breath, seal with a righteous kiss
> A dateless bargain to engrossing death.   (V.iii.113-6)

Has Shakespeare's eye at this moment fallen on a completed contract which lies at his elbow and has the pallour of the parchment and the redness of the wax given him this astonishing metaphor? Could the very wax, by some chance pressure of the ring, have taken the shape of a mouth? Was the contract one of engrossing? Shakespeare was

himself an engrosser, a gambler at Stratford in futures of barley in the
hope that a bad harvest would make barley scarce and raise its price
to a profit-making level. An engrossing contract would have dates, a
date for Shakespeare to pay the sum he was investing and a date for
the farmer or merchant to deliver the commodity. But the contract of
Romeo and Juliet with death is for eternity. It is ''dateless''. This is
not the only place where Shakespeare transmutes legal or business
terminology into poetry, *Sonnet XXX* is a striking example, but it is
surely the most poignant.

This notion, and we must remember its newness at the time, of
the sealing of a bond or contract of love with a kiss runs through the
whole of Shakespeare's works. Petruchio intends to marry
Katharine,

> And seal the title with a lovely kiss.
> (*The Taming of the Shrew* III.ii.121)

Julia and Proteus exchange rings and Julia suggests,

> And seal the bargain with a holy kiss.
> (*Two Gentlemen* II.ii.7)

Sadly, these bonds often do not hold, and Shakespeare uses the words
broken, cancelled, perjured, cracked for this source of human un-
happiness. He uses the word cracked five times to indicate the
severity of the rupture. The remembered beauty and the ultimate
pain of this experience are summed up in the lyric,

> Take, O take those lips away
>   That so sweetly were forsworn;
> And those eyes, the break of day,
>   Lights that do mislead the morn;
> But my kisses bring again, bring again,
> Seals of love, but sealed in vain, sealed in vain.
> (*Measure for Measure* IV.i.1-6)

More agonised is the cry of Troilus, for whom

> Cressida is mine, tied with the bonds of heaven . . .

but who now realises that

> The bonds of heaven are slipt, dissolved and loosed,
> And with another knot, five-finger-tied,
> The fractions of her faith, orts of her love,
> The fragments, scraps, the bits, and greasy relics
> Of her o'er-eaten faith, are bound to Diomed.
> (*Troilus and Cressida* V.ii.154-8)

Cressida has wriggled out of her bond and the sibilants, which often denote betrayal in Shakespeare, are his device here to suggest the nastiness of her action, in the words "slipt, dissolved and loosed". This is stressed by the worthless nature of the faith now bound, another bond, to Diomedes.

In the plays and poems there are at least twenty-five uses of the word contract for the swearing of oaths in love, betrothal or marriage. For Juliet things are moving too fast and she is afraid.

> Well, do not swear: although I joy in thee
> I have no joy of this contract tonight;
> It is too rash, too unadvised, too sudden . . .
> *(Romeo and Juliet* II.i.157-160)

And it is a contract which Theseus has in mind when he refers to his forthcoming wedding with Hippolyta as

> The sealing-day betwixt my love and me,
> For ever lasting bond of fellowship.
> *(Midsummer Night's Dream* I.i.84-5)

The word bond, for the relationship between lovers, between husband and wife, parent and child, friend and friend, occurs throughout, even in *The Merchant of Venice*, where an important bond, in the legal sense, is that held over Antonio by Shylock. And as we read through the plays we come upon bonds of faith (*Richard II* IV.i.76), of board and bed (*As You Like It* V.iv.148), of duty (*Henry VIII* III.ii.188), of friendship and of service. There is a bond of life in *Richard III* (IV.iv.77) and in *Cymbeline* (V.iv.28) and they are both to be cancelled.

Shakespeare sometimes uses band for bond. There is a band of truth (*All's Well* IV.ii.56), bands of life (*Richard II* II.ii.71), Hymen's bands (*As You Like It* V.iv. 135 and *Hamlet* III.ii.177-8) and bands in general (*I Henry IV* III.ii.157).

To Shakespeare these bonds were important because they represent the human relationships on which, if they are faithfully kept, we base a civilised way of life. But life is not simple, and a person involved in two perfectly acceptable bonds may find that they clash, to the destruction of his peace of mind and even of his life. When, in *Much Ado About Nothing*, Beatrice says, "Kill Claudio", it is not necessary to point out that the play moves abruptly towards the tragic. Benedick experiences an unforeseen and intense conflict of two loyalties. The dramatist has contrived a situation in which two essential bonds, of friendship and of love, pull in opposite directions, and we eagerly watch to see whether he can contrive to make these loyalties compatible. In so far as Benedick has ''qualities'' as a ''character'' they are there to give flesh and words to this agonising crisis.

So in the plays the bonds are in turn all tested; they come under different kinds of strain. If they withstand the strain and are restored, however near to cracking they have come, or if valuable new bonds are created, then we get what is usually called a comedy. If they break under the strain, so that life becomes impossible for the central character or characters, then we get what is called tragedy. Shakespeare showed little or no regard for academic classification and the division of his plays into comedies, histories and tragedies was made after his death, by more conventional friends and critics in the *First Folio* of 1623. The term romances for his last plays came much later and helps very little. The story of Suffolk and Margaret in *Henry VI Parts I and II*, almost entirely Shakespeare's invention in a so-called history play and therefore worthy of particular attention, this story, a play within a play, is utterly tragic. On the other hand, much of *Henry IV Parts I and II* is pure comedy, though again in a history play. Some of the plays, *Troilus and Cressida* being one, have such a confusion of broken and restored bonds that the critics have found them difficult to classify. These categories never hindered Shakespeare from writing as he wished, and are more apt to blind us than help us understand the plays, though they may offer a valid approach to Ben Jonson or Racine. There are as serious elements in *The Taming of the Shrew* and *Measure for Measure* as there are in *Macbeth* and *Coriolanus*, and the usual dismissal of *The Comedy of Errors* should not prevent us from seeing how close it comes to tragedy. Each and every one of these plays is a study of the bonds that bind us in human society.

Hamlet is an undubitably tragic play, with Hamlet himself the nodal centre of almost as many relationships as Shakespeare could give him, and all but one to be broken. At the beginning of the play his father is dead, murdered by his uncle, possibly with the connivance of his mother, to whom he is deeply attached. Here already are three important bonds cancelled. He is not given a brother or sister, but suspicion of the girl he loves leads to estrangement and her death. His schoolboy acquaintances, Rosencrantz and Guildenstern, betray him but he turns the tables on them. He is forced by circumstances into a quarrel with a friend, Laertes, and unwittingly kills him in a duel. He has been popular with the people, but the mob is behind

Laertes in their rebellious attack on the palace. It is clear that he himself, as well as the people of Denmark, expected him to come to the throne when his father died, but he tells us that his uncle has . . .

Popped in between the election and my hopes.

The bonds of love, family, acquaintance and state have thus all dissolved, but one bond still holds good, that of true friendship. Horatio stands by him to the end and is allowed to live on beyond the general carnage to speak well of Hamlet and to tell the truth about what has happened. This it is that saves the play from utter blackness, the unswerving fidelity of a friend. Friendship may well have been for Shakespeare the most important bond of all.

Hamlet was the victim of circumstances and of other people's actions, but another tragic figure, Richard III, himself cuts away the bonds which bind him to those about him, so that after a dream in which the ghosts of those he has destroyed come to reprove him he is reduced to saying,

Richard loves Richard; that is, I am I. (*Richard III* V.iii.185).

He has destroyed every link; he is no longer a lover, a husband, a relative, a friend. He is about to lose his throne and his life. No one but he himself loves him. He has become nothing and all he can say about himself is, ''I am . . . I'', as he clings to his last vestiges of identity, which are now slipping away from him. If all the bonds snap, and if no one any longer recognises us as brother, sister, parent, child, friend, fellow worker or any other of the possible relationships, then our identity disintegrates and we no longer have faith in what we think we are. The bonds are essential to our life and sanity.

The parent-child bond, particularly the father-daughter, was clearly of deep interest to Shakespeare and pertinent to his own life. With the return to Stratford in mind he brought this theme into his later plays, Lear and his disastrous handling of his three daughters, Leontes reunited with Perdita, Pericles with Marina, against the fearful background of the relationship between Antiochus and his own daughter; and the ultimate fantasy, Prospero's exclusive and isolated control of Miranda from babyhood to puberty. The father-son relationship, though occurring frequently in the plays, is not so intensely felt or important in the action, but in *Coriolanus* the dramatist plays one of his clever tricks with time, giving us in Young Marcius a picture of what his father must have been as a child and allowing us to realise how nature and upbringing combined to produce such an impatient, domineering person as Coriolanus.

In *Twelfth Night* there is no young child, no husband, wife, mother or father within the play, though marriages are forecast once the complications are ironed out. And these exclusions are deliberate. The dramatis personae fall into two groups, the two young men and two young women who will pair off neatly and a group of interesting peripheral people of uncertain age, Maria, Sir Toby, Sir Andrew, Malvolio, Fabian, Feste the Clown and Antonio the sea captain. Maria and Sir Toby will marry at a less romantic level than will the four young people, Sir Andrew and Malvolio would like to marry Olivia and Antonio is passionately devoted to Sebastian. The loves of these last three are unrequited, whilst Feste remains outside all this, with not even a bond of service assured, in contemplative loneliness. So there are different kinds of love relationships to be forged, sustained or denied, brother-sister love, healthy and normal in Viola and Sebastian, excessive and unhealthy in Olivia's pining for her dead brother. There is normal heterosexual love, growing unconsciously in Orsino and confused in Olivia, quite clear in Viola and Sebastian, and the homosexual love of Antonio for Sebastian, the latter regarding the sea captain as just a good friend. Malvolio suffers from excessive self-love, Sir Andrew is there for fun, whilst the more earthy union of Sir Toby and Maria has as good a chance of success as any.

I have implied that the exclusions as well as the choice of relationships to be dealt with in any of these plays of Shakespeare are deliberately planned, the persons carefully selected for the working out of the theme, the set of bonds which in any one play are to be exemplified, to be tested, to be allowed to clash and some-times to disintegrate, persons who are often such realistic and complex puppets that critics have been tempted to treat them as human beings. Here the consideration of sources, where sources are apparent, becomes far from a dry-as-dust academic exercise. If Shakespeare uses a story already told, then what he omits, uses and adds to the material quite clearly reveals his intentions. And the very choice of a story to use may indicate a search on his part for a vehicle in which to analyse a particular set of relationships. The shipwreck on the magic island of *The Tempest* gave the dramatist more themes than the father-daughter bond. There were contemporary situations and relationships which called for his comment; King James, who like Prospero spent too much time in his study and delegated power to favourites; and there were the plantations in America which had created a new relationship for western Europeans, that between colonist and native, shadowed in Prospero and Caliban. *The Tempest* offers many other possibilities of interpretation. Caliban and Ariel may be taken as necessary, contrasting poles within the invented personality of Prospero and the real one of Shakespeare himself. And the magic island where Prospero had such power, and which he was now leaving to return to the business of government, was the London theatre the dramatist was now leaving for Stratford.

All these bonds, of service, friendship, love and marriage, are seen by Shakespeare as contracts which should not be broken or easily cancelled (''love's long since cancelled woe''). The infidelity of a wife was abhorrent to him and rarely occurs in the plays and poems. Jealousy, or the usually unjust suspicion that a bond is cracking, is the terribly destructive force we see at work in *Othello* and *The Winter's Tale*. The first kiss of love is the red-lipped seal on as potentially binding a document as the law or human decency can deliver, as binding as wax and a signature on parchment, the handshake of friendship or the unspoken, unwritten bond of consanguinity.

Sea-storm, Tide Imagery and Mutiny in Shakespeare

An interesting complex of images in Shakespeare's writing associates tumultuous behaviour of the sea with mutiny, usurpation and riotous behaviour of a rabble. The culmination of this set of associations is, not surprisingly, to be found in *The Tempest*, where usurpation of authority and a storm at sea are basic to the action.

> *Boatswain:* . . . What cares these roarers for the name of king? . . .
> You are a counsellor; if you can command these elements to silence,
> and work the peace of the moment, we will not hand a rope more; use
> your authority.   (I.i. 16-17, 20-23)

The idea of roaring insurrection threatening authority is carried on in the next scene, where Ariel describes the storm.

> . . . the fire, and cracks,
> Of sulphurous roaring, the most mighty Neptune
> Seem to besiege, and make his bold waves tremble,
> Yea, his dread trident shake.   (I.ii.201-204)

A little later we have "contentious waves" (II.i.118) and then towards the end of the play the idea is taken up once more, this time by Prospero.

> . . . . I have bedimm'd
> The noontide sun, call'd forth the mutinous winds,
> And twixt the green sea and the azured vault
> Set roaring war.   (V.i.43-6)

Once more a storm, mutiny and roaring, The "calm seas, auspicious gales" of Prospero's last speech go with the restitution of his authority in his dukedom and the pardoning of his deceivers.

But these same associations run right through Shakespeare's work, dramatic and poetic, from the beginning to the end. In the storm at sea in *Othello*,

> The chiding billows seems to pelt the clouds.   (II.i.12)

Here in the verb to pelt, there is the suggestion of the stone-throwing of a riotous mob. Ulysses, in his speech on the collapse of order and degree, exclaims,

> .... what mutiny,
> What raging of the sea...   (*Troil. & Cress.* I.iii.96)

and later in the same speech his example from nature of the result of loss of degree is,

> .... the bounded waters
> Should lift their bosoms higher than the shores
> And make a sop of all this solid globe.   (I.iii.111-113)

This is not so much a storm as a flood image, of a type to be referred to later, but the idea is that of the usurpation of authority.

The mutiny in Tarquin's blood carries echoes, or rather forecasts, of the sea-storms of the plays.

> His eye, which late this mutiny restrains,
> Unto a greater uproar tempts his veins.   (*Lucrece* 426-7)

Here authority itself, represented by Tarquin's eye, seems to join in the insurrection of the tide of blood. Two stanzas later Tarquin is called ''a foul usurper''. But the image is used in a reverse sense soon afterwards, when Lucrece pleads with Tarquin.

> Be moved with my tears, my sighs, my groans:

> All which together, like a troubled ocean,
> Beat at thy rocky and wrack-threatening heart
> To soften it with their continual motion... (589-591)

A troubled ocean is very different from a stormy sea and here the motion of the sea is gentle and continuous, in accordance with the protective associations of the sea which are to be seen, for instance, in *Richard II,* II.i.40-63, where also we have,

> England, bound in with the triumphant sea,
> Whose rocky shore beats back the envious siege
> Of watery Neptune... (61-63)

In *King John*, too, England ...

> ....that white-faced shore
> Whose foot spurns back the ocean's roaring tides.   (II.i.23-4)

Here the roaring tides are advancing enemies and the word

usurpation occurs only a few lines earlier. The "white-faced shore" is not only the cliffs of Dover but a suggestion of the fear felt by one whose authority is threatened.

Not only storms at sea but also the flooding of the tide is linked with mutiny and usurpation in Shakespeare's mind. The furrowed brow of a messenger who brings news of the failure of a rebellion to a participant is brilliantly likened to the lines left in the sand by the receding tide.

> So looks the strond whereupon the imperious flood
> Hath left a witness'd usurpation.   (*2 Henry IV* I.i.62)

The ebbing of the tide symbolises the collapse of the insurrection and the wrinkles in the sand the worries that face the defeated rebels.

Antony says to the listening crowd which he is about to turn into a destructive rabble,

> . . . . let me not stir you up
> To such a sudden flood of mutiny.   (*Jul. Caes.* III.ii.214-5)

In *Hamlet* the revolt of Laertes is compared to the tidal flooding of low country.

> The ocean, overpeering of his list
> Eats not the flats with more impetuous haste
> Than young Laertes, in a riotous head,
> O'erbears your officers.   (IV.v.100-103)

That Shakespeare had actually seen the sea behave in this fashion is vouched for by Sonnet 64.

> When I have seen the hungry ocean gain
> Advantage on the kingdom of the shore. . .

Here the word *kingdom* evokes the idea of insurrection, of usurpation, linked with the destructive flooding or erosion of the land.

A tide-rabble association occurs in *Henry VIII*, where a noisy mob breaks into the palace yard. The Porter asks,

> Is this a place to roar in?

And then,

> How got they in, and be hang'd?

His man answers,

> Alas, I know not; how gets the tide in?   (V.iii.7 ff.)

The rushing of the tide through a gap occurs in another tide-rabble image in *Troilus and Cressida*.

> .... if you give way,
> Or hedge aside from the direct forthright,
> Like to an enter'd tide, they all rush by
> And leave you hindmost.   (III.iii.157-160)

A similar use of the image is made in *Coriolanus* to describe the Roman rabble celebrating the triumph of Volumnia over her son and the collapse of Marcius' insurrection.

> Ne'er through an arch so hurried the blown tide
> As the recomforted through the gates.   (V.v.50-51)

Shakespeare had already used this image of tidal water rushing through an arch, with swirling waters eddying back, in *Lucrece*, to express the conflict of emotions in the breast of Collatine.

> As through an arch the violent roaring tide
> Outruns the eye that doth behold his haste,
> Yet in the eddy boundeth in his pride
> Back to the strait that forced him on so fast.   (1667-1670)

In all these cases the associations are of sea-storm and tidal flooding with mutiny, insurrection, usurpation of authority, and with an extension of the meaning to the mutiny in the blood and the kind of civil war that goes on in a disturbed mind.

Shakespeare has told us that he has observed the ocean "gain advantage" on the shore, and the picture of Laertes' insurrection in *Hamlet* seems to suggest either Lancashire or the East Coast. He has been appalled at the speed with which the tide rises on a low coast and fascinated by the furrows left on the surface of the sand by the ebbing water.

The image of the cliff which resists the attack of the waves, but which is sometimes eaten away by them, may or may not spring from actual observation, but the frequency of the image in his work and the particularity of the cliff description in *King Lear* (IV.vi.14-27) suggests a personal experience. After all, Dover was not far from London for a man who regularly rode down to Stratford.

For the rushing of the tide through an arch Shakespeare had to go no further than London Bridge. There he observed the eddying return of some of the .water, which he mentions in *Lucrece* and the increased speed of the water when the wind was behind it, a fact familiar to oarsmen, the "blown tide" of *Coriolanus*.

But the sea-storm-mutiny association is surely of literary provenance. Here that most unusual extended simile in the *Aeneid* comes to mind, where Vergil reverses the usual process by taking an image from human behaviour to describe a natural phenomenon.

Ac veluti magno in populo cum saepe coorta est
Seditio saevitque animis ignobile volgus
Iamque faces et saxa volant, furor arma ministrat,
Tum pietate gravem ac mentis si forte virum quem
Conspexere, silent arrectisque auribus adstant,
Ille regit dictis animos et pectora mulcet:
Sic cunctus pelagi cecidit fragor.   (I.148-154)

''It had been like a sudden riot in some great assembly, when, as they will, the meaner folk forget themselves and grow violent, so that firebrands and stones are soon flying, for savage passion quickly finds weapons. But then they may chance to see some man whose character and record command their respect. If so, they will wait in silence, listening keenly. He will speak to them, calming their passions and guiding their energies. So, now, all the uproar of the ocean subsided.'' (Penguin ed. Trans. W.F.Jackson Knight, p.32)

The riotous rabble is there, the pelting of stones, the roaring; then the reassertion of authority. All this is likened to a storm at sea, an image of which Shakespeare was to make such rich and varied use.

The Taming of the Shrew

In a 1978 production of *The Taming of the Shrew* at Stratford, directed by Michael Bogdanov, a transformed Induction was really made to lead into a play, though not in any way suggested by Shakespeare. Christopher Sly was made to become Petruchio. He appeared in the auditorium; quarrelled noisily with an usherette, jumped on to the stage and systematically destroyed the pretty Italianate décor the audience had been looking at since they took their seats. People who had not been let into the secret were greatly alarmed by this apparent vandalism. In this way Petruchio was allowed to establish his attitude towards the conventions, and the violence of his methods, whilst the trick played on Christopher Sly was completely dropped. This was an ingenious, if shocking, opening to the play, which used rather than interpreted the Induction. Shakespeare, for that matter, abandoned Sly and the trick played on him at the end of the play, so that *The Taming of the Shrew* is not a play within a play, a situation which would have taken it one more remove from reality. If Shakespeare was here rehashing an old play, what justification had he for retaining Sly? If the dramatist invented him, why did he not return to him at the end of the play? If no justification for Sly and his hoodwinking can be seen then the play can be acted, as has in fact happened, without the Induction, and appear to suffer no loss save that of some unrelated fun.

What happens in this Induction, which is in two scenes? An unnamed Lord returns from hunting, showing an interest in his hounds equal to that of Theseus in *Midsummer Night's Dream*. Outside an alehouse near his residence he finds the drunken Christopher Sly noisily asleep. He immediately decides to carry out what he calls ''a pastime passing excellent'' on him, a trick which turns out to be a psychological experiment.

> Sirs, I will practise on this drunken man.
> What think you, if he were conveyed to bed,
> Wrapped in sweet clothes, rings put upon his fingers,
> A most delicious banquet by his bed
> And brave attendants near him when he wakes,
> Would not the beggar then forget himself?   (Ind. i.35-40)

He gives careful and detailed instructions, saying that it must be "husbanded with modesty", for he wants the trick to succeed.

Now, aptly as in *Hamlet*, a company of strolling players appears on the scene. The Lord greets them much as Hamlet does the later troupe and they agree to take part in his device, swearing to keep a straight face.

> Fear not, my lord; we can contain ourselves
> Were he the veriest antick in the world.   (i.99-100)

Bartholemew the page must, unwillingly, dress up as Sly's lady wife. The trick works, though Sly makes a brave effort to cling to his identity, a plain Englishman placed suddenly in aristocratic surroundings. He protests,

> What, would you make me mad? Am not I Christopher
> Sly, old Sly's son of Burton-heath; by birth a
> pedlar, by education a card-maker, by transmutation
> a bear-herd, and now by present profession a tinker?
> Ask Marian Hacket, the fat ale-wife of Wincot, if
> she knows me not... What, I am not bestraught: here's...
>   (ii.17-25)

But there is no one within sight prepared to vouch for his old identity or support him in his refusal to accept this new one. If no one recognises us for what we think we are, how long can we continue to believe it ourselves?

The vacuum created by the disintegration of an identity is easier to fill, for it must be filled. Sly accepts the judgement of those around him.

> Am I a lord, and have I such a lady,
> Or do I dream? Or have I dreamed till now?
> I do not sleep, I see, I hear, I speak,
> I smell sweet savours and I feel soft things.
> Upon my life I am a lord indeed
> And not a tinker, not Christophero Sly.
> Well, bring our lady hither to our sight,
> And, once again, a pot o'the smallest ale.   (ii.68-75)

His identity has changed, but not his personality or his tastes. He still prefers beer to sack and, when his page-wife is presented to him, all the old rural bluntness is there. A rough rural philosophy too.

> Come madam wife, sit by my side,
> And let the world slip. We shall ne'er be younger. (ii.112-4)

He shows a healthy directness too.

> Madam, undress you and come now to bed.

But he is persuaded to postpone the pleasures of the bed and he agrees to watch the play.

This Induction has shown us how quickly a person will settle down to a new identity. That is its purpose, to warn us to look out for changes of identity in the play which is now about to begin. And changes of identity we will find, at more than one level; that is the theme of the play, not just the subjugation of a woman by a man.

Lucentio, a young gentleman of Pisa, has come to Padua to study,

> ... and haply institute
> A course of learning and ingenious studies. (I.i.8-9)

His servant, Tranio, who seems to be equally well educated, does not accept this concentration upon the things of the mind.

> Let's be no stoicks nor no stocks, I pray;
> Or so devote to Aristotle's ethics
> As Ovid be an outcast quite abjured. (I.i.31-3)

The matter is settled out of hand, for now Baptista, a wealthy Paduan, appears with his two daughters, followed by two suitors. To all appearances, and her father accepts these appearances, Bianca, the younger sister, is quiet, obedient and devoted to music and poetry. Her father insists that she shall not marry until her elder sister, Katharina, is disposed of, and since Katharina is a known shrew there seems to be little prospect of this happening. To keep Bianca at home Baptista requires tutors for her, and this gives Lucentio his opportunity, for he has already, at first sight, fallen in love with her.

> Tranio, I burn, I pine, I perish, Tranio,
> If I achieve not this young modest girl. (I.i.154-5)

(Is the young gallant acting the part of a lover here, in these exaggerated terms, or is this really a thunderbolt of love?) Between them, master and man now think of a trick to gain Lucentio admission to Bianca. Lucentio will offer himself as a teacher, whilst Tranio will become Lucentio in Padua. No one knows them here and they immediately exchange clothes, for dress has a good deal to do with identity. For Lucentio this is a temporary expedient and once alone with Bianca he can be himself again. Tranio enters much more fully into his new identity and, given the opportunity, could flourish in the new role of master. He deceives Baptista into accepting him as the true Lucentio and suitor to Bianca.

There is yet another assumed identity to come, when an old Pedant travelling from Mantua, is frightened into accepting the role of Vincentio, Lucentio's father, who has come to see how his son is faring, in order to speed up the courtship of Bianca by Lucentio. This Pedant enters fully into the deception and has the effrontery to sustain it in the face of Vincentio himself. Tranio and Biondello pretend not to know Vincentio and, alone in a strange city and denied by people he knows, he comes nearest to tragedy. (A similar danger occurs to a father in *The Comedy of Errors*.) But the bond between father and son is too strong for Lucentio to deny his father and this piety saves the old man from perturbation of mind and possible imprisonment. In the meantime Petruchio has arrived from Verona, has swept aside Katharina's shrewishness and has gone off to Venice for wedding clothes.

So we are asked to believe that Bianca is the shy, modest girl who turns shrew as soon as she is married, for that is what the play appears to show. But is this so? When she first appears, Lucentio sees in her "maid's mild behaviour and sobriety" and she puts on an act of complete obedience to her father. She is certainly dominated by her elder sister but she shows sharp spirit and independence when Hortensio and Lucentio quarrel over which of them shall give her the first lesson.

> I am no breeching scholar in the schools,
> I'll not be tied to hours, nor 'pointed times,
> But learn my lessons as I please myself.   (III.i.18-20)

This is not the sort of outburst she would allow her father to hear and it should have warned Lucentio. She takes Lucentio's hidden declaration calmly, even encourages him and is soon ready to discuss the Art of Love with him.

> And may you prove, sir, master of your art.   (IV.ii.9)

Once safely married she shows what I take to have been her true nature all along, in flatly refusing her husband's first request.

In contrast to Bianca, Katharina has made a convincing show as a bad-tempered creature from childhood and she is notorious in Padua for "her scolding tongue". But the verbal and physical rough-and-tumble of her first meeting with Petruchio almost silences her, so that her father finds her "in her dumps". When Petruchio sweeps out with the words

> And kiss me, Kate; we will be married a' Sunday   (II.i.317)

she is given no word of protest. What can have happened? The answer comes from Petruchio, when he says to her father,

> ... yourself and all the world
> That talked of her have talked amiss of her.
> If she be curst, it is for policy,
> For she's not froward, but modest as the dove;
> She is not hot, but temperate as the morn...   (II.i.285-9)

This is exaggerated and there is double talk here. When we remember Katharina's behaviour and observe her reception of this speech, we must laugh at its absurdity. But it is possible that Petruchio knows what he is saying and that he has perceived or sensed another Katharina behind the termagant mask. The fact is that this behaviour of Katharina's has kept her free from a number of undesired suitors, thereby protecting her from being given by her father to a man she does not love. Now here suddenly is a handsome young stranger who claims to find her beautiful. Her assumed identity of a scold, which has worked well in childhood and young womanhood, all the tantrums and scalding words, can now be dropped. They have fulfilled their function. Her silence for several minutes before Petruchio leaves for Venice, or perhaps a pause in the wrestling and verbal match a little earlier, may be the time when this realisation comes to her. She is already won. Why then does Shakespeare make Petruchio continue to heap torments and indignities upon her? Was her submission so sudden and so apparently out of character 'that Petruchio needs to confirm his mastery and be quite sure? Did it occur to the dramatist as he wrote that the part of Katharina would be played by a boy and that a boy could take it, so that the farcical slapstick is allowed to continue to get laughs and not to make it all seem too easy for the girl? And does Katharina's long final speech, which many find embarrassing, swing too far in the opposite direction from her shrewishness? Can we be allowed to think that she is again playing a part, acting a new identity, and that their marriage will in fact settle down to a Beatrice and Benedick kind of association?

What of Petruchio? We know nothing about him until his arrival in Padua and then only that he is of good birth, that his father is dead and that he is looking for a rich wife. He is not known in Padua, so may this swashbuckling roughness of his be an assumed identity too, an *ad hoc* device to deal with a wealthy, attractive young termagant? May he then, having sensed her interest in him and her possible submission, have gone on behaving in the rough manner which has worked, either out of pleasure in an acted part which staggers everyone or just in case his instincts have misinformed him? Apart from the Induction Shakespeare gives us little to go on and we are forced to ask these questions. But the dramatist has exemplified for us, through his puppets, how we adopt identities, or have them thrust upon us. The world is, in the words of Antonio of Venice,

> A stage where every man must play a part..,

a statement which can be read as meaning that we are required to pretend to be something besides what we really are. We all do this to some degree, sometimes in our choice of the clothes we wear, how we do our hair, our stance and gait, even in the cultivated expressions on our faces. There are people who practise these before a glass, just like actors before they go on to the stage. We wish to be thought this or that kind of person and we act these parts so long as we find them successful, and we abandon them under the test of a crisis, a first job, marriage, some profound clash of impulses or loyalties, or even on the death-bed.

There was no need for Shakespeare to show us Christopher Sly restored to his identity as a drunken tinker. Sly had no hope of continuing to live the life of a lord, as Tranio might have had, nor would he have been happy in such a role, as Tranio would. He has played his part in suggesting to us what we should look out for in the play and how we should regard the people about us in our daily life. *The Taming of the Shrew* is an enlightening psychological document.

The Comedy of Errors Rescued from Tragedy

There is no need to insist on or to exemplify the way in which *The Comedy of Errors* has until recently been considered a farce. Coleridge thought it so and on the stage the play has usually been taken as a romp.[1] (Shakespeare producers must have their secret list of comedies which may or may not be taken as pantomime.) A careful analysis of this play, however, shows that it might easily have worked out as a tragedy.

Shakespeare criticism has from Meres to the present day been misled by the pedantic division of drama into comedy or tragedy. Even Dr Johnson, who admitted the appeal from criticism to nature, who observed the mingling of the comic and the serious in everyday life and who said, "Shakespeare's plays are not in the rigorous sense either tragedies or comedies, but compositions of a distinct kind, exhibiting the real state of sublunary nature",[2] even such a perceptive mind was too steeped in conventional ways of thinking not to protest occasionally against incongruities he found in Shakespeare's plays.

The incongruities in *The Comedy of Errors* have side-tracked the critics, who have preferred to consider the play as a farce which is spoilt by the injudicious introduction of serious material. Dowden was perhaps the most sympathetic in seeing the approach to tragedy in the play. For Quiller-Couch the play fell to the ground between farce and romance.[3] To H.B. Charlton the introduction of the serious characters, Egeon, Luciana and Emilia, brings in "a range of sentiment incompatible with the atmosphere of *The Comedy of Errors*", where the general temper of life is "crude, coarse and brutal" in his opinion.[4] G.R. Elliott seems to have been nearer to full appreciation of the nature of the play in contrasting the comic horror of mistaken identity with "the real horror of the complete identity of two human

beings.''[5] R.A. Foakes discusses more fully than has previously been
done the serious elements in the play, the loss and rediscovery of
identity, the idea of madness in this connection, the resulting ''disruption of family, personal and social relationships'',[6] witchcraft,
and concludes: ''The fact is that the serious elements are in some
danger of going unobserved, while no one is likely to miss the fun,
especially in the distorted and jazzed-up versions of the play which
are commonly staged.''

It may be opportune to look further into these serious elements
and the apparent incongruity that has been seen in the play. A further
analysis of the play seems called for, so that the reason may emerge
for Shakespeare's addition of the two Dromios to the material he took
from Plautus. This in turn may throw some light on the famous
incongruities.

It will then appear that Shakespeare's purpose in making this
duplication was not merely to increase the comic effect by repetition
of a situation on a lower plane, a device he frequently used in comedy; it was not even to enhance the fun which could be elicited from
the mistaking of identities. It was to save the play as comedy, to
ensure, in fact, that there should be fun at all.

As Shakespeare conceived the situation of Antipholus of Syracuse, the young man's bewilderment might well have made him
desperate and against the solemn background of Egeon's predicament any act of violence could have carried Antipholus on to tragedy.
On the other hand, this might have been precipitated by Antipholus
of Ephesus, the more violent of the twins. The two Dromios, however, not only provide the low humour, the backchat, the healthy
indecencies; not only is their predicament kept firmly comic, but the
occasional contact with Dromio of Syracuse, the only person in the
play (before the final recognition by Egeon) who recognizes him for
what he is, clearly saves the sanity of Antipholus of Syracuse. It is true
that his meetings with Dromio of Ephesus confuse him further but
they do enable him to work off some of his mental anguish in the
physical drubbings he administers.

Without the two Dromios the play would hardly have had any
farcical elements, except for the late introduction of Dr Pinch, who is
apt to be blown up into a music-hall act, not entirely without justification from the text. Much less a farce, the play might not even have
ended as a comedy. After all, Antipholus of Ephesus had much more
to go on than Othello was to have.[7]

It may be worthwhile going quickly through the play once more, to follow this thread of concern with identity, to establish the seriousness of this thread and to observe how the two Dromios, more particularly Dromio of Syracuse, pull the play back from the brink of disaster.

Act I sc. i. Egeon's identification with Syracuse threatens to cause his death. (The dangers of peripheral aspects of identity.)

The Duke's sympathy is hamstrung by his own identity as ruler (ll.142-5).

Act I sc. ii. Antipholus of Syracuse must deny one part of his identity, his Syracusan origin, to preserve his goods (ll.1-2).

To the losses he has already suffered he now foresees the possible complete loss of his identity. This is expressed in the telling image of the drop of water:

> I to the world am like a drop of water
> That in the ocean seeks another drop,
> Who, falling there to find his fellow forth,
> Unseen, inquisitive, confounds himself.
> So I, to find a mother and a brother,
> In quest of them, unhappy, lose myself.   (ll.35-40)

Dromio of Ephesus now appears and confuses him. He puts this down to witchcraft.

Act II sc. i. According to Luciana, the personality and will of a woman should be subjugated to that of her husband. Men, she says,

> Are masters to their females, and their lords:
> Then let your will attend on their accords.   (ll.24-5)

(Katharina says something very similar at the end of *The Taming of the Shrew*, when she has become a quite different person from the girl everyone knew and whom we saw at the beginning of the play.)

Act II sc. ii. Antipholus of Syracuse desperately tries to find reasons for the new identity which is being thrust upon him. In Act I it was witchcraft; now it is dreams.

> What, was I married to her in my dream?   (l.182)

Antipholus and Dromio of Syracuse are forced to acknowledge that some change has come over them, but the similarity of their experience is a kind of comfort. A puzzling experience which is shared is not so alarming as one faced alone. Antipholus of Syracuse now sees the change as a mental one.

> *Syr. Dro.*   I am transformed, master, am I not?
> *Syr. Ant.*   I think thou art in mind, and so am I.   (ll.195-6)

A little later, as he goes in to dine with Adriana, Antipholus of Syracuse for the moment accepts his recognition by others as a person who is strange to himself. It may be worth while risking an adventure in another identity:

> Am I in earth, in heaven, or in hell?
> Sleeping or waking, mad or well advis'd?
> Known unto these, and to myself disguis'd,
> I'll say as they say, and persever so,
> And in this mist at all adventures go.   (ll.212-16)

Act III sc. i. It is now the turn of Antipholus of Ephesus; he is denied by his wife:

> *Adriana:* Your wife, sir knave? go, get you from the door.   (l.64)

Dromio of Ephesus is similarly refused entrance and he also has a wife in the house. Antipholus of Ephesus is only restrained from immediate violence by the two puzzled merchants.

Act III sc. ii. Falling in love with Luciana creates a new human bond for Antipholus of Syracuse to replace those he has lost. The trouble is that this seems to involve the acceptance of a new identity and, still in the adventurous mood in which he went in to dine with his twin brother's wife, he invites Luciana to undertake his education as a new person.

> Teach me, dear creature, how to think and speak;
> Lay open to my earthy gross conceit,
> Smother'd in errors, feeble, shallow, weak,
> The folded meaning of your words' deceit ...
> Are you a god? would you create me new?
> Transform me then, and to your power I'll yield.
>   (ll.33-6 and 39-40)

But he has not yet completely abandoned his personality, the identity he knows and clings to, and the use of the word 'deceit' in reference to her words stresses his awareness of the dangerous falsity of the situation. The succeeding lines go,

> But if that I am I, then well I know
> Your weeping sister is no wife of mine.   (ll.41-2)

Even to win this lovely girl he has no wish to lose his identity. It is an extreme version of the surrender of independence which to some extent love always demands. It is a tense situation for him and by no means funny. Dromio of Syracuse also wonders whether he is himself and is surprised to be recognized by his master:

> *Syr. Dro.*   Do you know me, sir? Am I Dromio? Am I your man?
> Am I myself?   (1.72)

When his questions have been satisfactorily answered by his master, Dromio can afford to be funny at the expense of the fat wife who has been foisted on to him. But no comedy, only a rather nasty situation, sprang from Adriana's mistaking of Antipholus of Syracuse for her husband.

At this point Antipholus and Dromio of Syracuse decide to leave Ephesus:

> *Syr. Ant.*   If everyone knows us and we know none,
> 'Tis time to trudge, pack and be gone.   (ll.151-2)

For Antipholus the only temptation to remain is Luciana, whom he now regards as a witch, relating her to the Sirens of the *Odyssey*.

> But her fair sister . . .
> Hath almost made me traitor to myself;
> But lest myself be guilty to self-wrong,
> I'll stop mine ears against the mermaid's song.   (ll.158-161-3)

To love Luciana would be a form of suicide of the identity, since it would involve acceptance of a new one. At this point Angelo enters with the chain ordered by Antipholus of Ephesus:

> *Angelo:*   Master Antopholus.
> *Syr. Ant.*   Ay, that's my name.   (ll.163-4)

"That's my name", but not, "I'm the person you're looking for?" The name now seems to have no relation to the person, a disturbing dissociation.

Act IV sc. iii. Antipholus of Syracuse, owing to the confusion of the two Dromios, is still at Ephesus, showered with gifts and compliments from people he does not know, and still putting it all down to sorcery.

> *Syr. Ant.*   There's not a man I meet but doth salute me
> As if I were their well-acquainted friend,
> And every one doth call me by my name . . .
> Sure these are but imaginary wiles,
> And Lapland sorcerers inhabit here.   (ll.1-3 and 10-11)

But he seems to be more confident of his identity now and less fearful
of losing it. It is a city of illusions, a place notorious for witchcraft,
and the sooner he and his man are out of it the better.

> And here we wander in illusions—
> Some blessed power deliver us from hence!   (ll.41-2)

Departure from the city would restore him to what he was before the
beginning of the play, but it would, of course, mean death for his
father. The other Antipholus's violent attack upon his wife (Act IV
sc. iv. ll.99-104) shows how dangerous this confusion of identities has
become and how near to tragedy the central characters are brought.

In Act V the explanation is unwound and all identities are
restored, but not before the Duke has commented:

> I think you all have drunk of Circe's cup.   (l.271)

The confusion of identity has been painful and potentially dangerous for the two Antipholuses. The denial of identity has been most
complete for Antipholus of Syracuse, but he is in a foreign country, in
a city renowned for witchcraft and sorcery, and he clings to his reason
by reminding himself of this fact. He can always get away and this he
is always on the point of doing. For Antipholus of Ephesus the case is
very different. He is in a town where has been a person of importance
for twenty years. Quite suddenly to have his orders disregarded by his
servant, to be refused admission to his own house and to be denied by
his own wife in broad daylight in the presence of others, to be arrested
for debt and to be treated as a madman, all this makes a galling,
infuriating experience for the Ephesian twin. He is a more violent
character than his brother and he might quite easily have killed his
wife.

It is significant that the person of Antipholus of Syracuse
becomes much more important in Shakespeare's play than his
counterpart in the source play by Plautus. Luciana is an addition to
the story and so is the introduction of Egeon into the action. The
possibilties of the story which interested Shakespeare, his recasting of
it and the new elements he introduced, all led headlong towards
tragedy, but he may not have felt sufficiently confident at this stage in
his career as a dramatist to allow this to happen. It might have been
thought too outrageous a flouting of a classical model at a time when
Shakespeare was in open competition with university wits. (A similar
hesitation, though in the reverse direction, is observable on Shakespeare's part in *Romeo and Juliet*, which has all the elements and

atmosphere of comedy until the death of Mercutio, an event which the dramatist had reluctantly to bring about in order to give the play the promised tragic ending.)

The Comedy of Errors is an early study in the nature of personal identity. How soon does one's conception of oneself, the belief in one's own identity, break down before lack of recognition on the part of others? How far do we need others in order to have an identity at all? Is one's identity entirely dependent on the personal and social links and bonds, the ties of family, love, friendship and civic duty? In order that these questions might be tackled without in this case leading to madness and violent death, as they do in *King Lear*, Shakespeare added the twin servants. To condemn this on the grounds of improbability, as Quiller-Couch does, undersigned by Dover Wilson,[8] is to apply a standard which would not occur to one in the theatre, which is not relevant to drama or to great art of any kind. Shakespeare himself joked about this sort of criticism. "If this were play'd upon a stage now, I could condemn it as an improbable fiction."[9] It is curiously naïve to require more verisimilitude on the stage than is to be observed in life. Or perhaps absurdly sophisticated. The two Dromios of course provide a lot of fun, but this is not their main function. Whilst more often than not they unwittingly add to the confusion, they do sometimes recognize their true masters and the analysis made above shows this to be the only link that Antipholus of Syracuse has with his remembered identity, with reality. The fact that his servant is also taken for another person extends the predicament outside himself and makes it possible for him to hold the theory of witchcraft as a cause, thereby savig his reason. Antipholus of Ephesus, whom Shakespeare makes less interesting and sympathetic, is not given this comfort, for there is little consolation for him in the fact that his servant is also refused admission to their house. This simply confirms the treachery of his wife to his mind.

There is an interesting ambivalence in the use made of Luciana.[10] At a moment when Antipholus of Syracuse's identity seems to be disintegrating and he is in danger of losing all links with his past life, his new love for Luciana promises the building of a new bond, a new relationship to compensate for the loss of the old. But since a new identity is also involved, which is only viable in relation to her, this would be an act of treachery to his past and to the identity to which he is still clinging. Luciana is therefore a siren and a witch seducing him from his true self.

What seems to have happened in Shakespeare's handling of the story is this. He found the predicament of Antipholus of Syracuse far from farcical, but rather an opportunity to probe into the nature of personal identity. To provide another view of the problem he added to the story the ordeal of Egeon and his denial by Antipholus and Dromio of Ephesus, who of course do not know him but whom the old man takes to be those of Syracuse. The function of Luciana has already been discussed. The incongruities which have been seen in the play may be said to arise from Shakespeare's failure to accommodate the elements that really interested him in the play to a dramatic formula from which he could not yet quite escape. But since his additions to the story must indicate the nature and direction of his interest we should surely pay more attention to the serious elements in the play, without any risk, as R.A. Foakes points out, of surrendering any of the fun it offers. The Clowns in *Hamlet* are not the less funny for our considering the play to be in the main serious, nor would we enjoy the two Dromios and Dr Pinch the less for a fuller realization of the significance of Antipholus of Syracuse.

This is not to read something into the play which is not there but to find conspicuously laid out in it a concern which is central to the writing and thought of our mid-twentieth century, the whole matter of the nature of personal identity, the study of which in *The Comedy of Errors* was kept by Shakespeare on a comic level only by the introduction of the two Dromios.

---

[1] For a summing up of views on the play see R.A. Foakes, *The Comedy of Errors*, Introduction, Arden edition (1962).

[2] *Johnson on Shakespeare*, ed. Raleigh (1908), p. 15.

[3] *The Comedy of Errors*, Introduction, New Cambridge edition (1962), p. xxiv.

[4] *Shakespearean Comedy* (1938), p. 70.

[5] Foakes, op. cit., p. xliii.

[6] Foakes op. cit., p. xlix.

[7] J.R. Brown suggests in *Shakespeare and his Comedies* (1957) p. 57, another kind of seriousness, apart from considerations of identity. "No one would argue that *The Comedy of Errors* is a very profound play, but reference to Shakespeare's ideas about love's wealth and its difference from commercial wealth does suggest that is action is not merely that of a merry-go-round."

[8] *Errors*, Introduction (1962).

[9] *Twelfth Night*, III.iv.ll.127-8.

[10] Luciana is in a sense a step towards the heroines of the later romantic comedies, but she stands apart in the unusually equivocal situation Shakespeare gives her.

Suffolk and Margaret: A Study of Some Sections of Shakespeare's *Henry VI*

The illicit love affair which Shakespeare gave to Queen Margaret and the Earl (afterward Duke) of Suffolk in *1* and *2 Henry VI* is unhistorical. At a time when Shakespeare for his dramatic purposes was ruthlessly simplifying and trimming history, he chose to invent this tragic and, to most people, disagreeable love story, basing his invention only on some hints in Hall's *Chronicle*. There appears to have been no demanding reason, dramatically, for this invention, even though it does link together *Parts 1* and *2* to a degree which makes them seem one play. Some other situation, vouched for by history, could have done this equally well. When Shakespeare omitted or cut material from a source he was using, the dramatic purpose of the omission or cutting down is usually clear to us. But when he enlarged or invented on the basis of a hint and if there is no conspicuous dramatic need for the innovation, then one may be allowed to suspect a particular interest on Shakespeare's part in this addition to the story.

Let us look closely at the relationship between Princess Margaret, later Queen of England, and Suffolk as given by Shakespeare. In *1 Henry VI*, V.iii, the French are defeated and Joan la Pucelle is taken prisoner by the Duke of York. Margaret becomes, unhistorically, Suffolk's prisoner. Before he knows who she is, he is impressed by her beauty. He enters, dragging her by the hand, ''Be what thou wilt, thou art my prisoner'' (l.45). [2] She has clearly been protesting her importance. He pauses to look at her:

> O fairest beauty, do not fear, nor fly,
> For I will touch thee but with reverent handes:
> I kiss these fingers for eternal peace
> And lay them gently on thy tender side.
> Who art thou? Say, that I may honour thee. (ll.46-50)

She gives him her name and rank and he replies with his. Then follows a curious Wooing Scene in which Suffolk fights a delaying action while he works a plan to win her for himself:

> Be not offended, nature's miracle,
> Thou art allotted to be ta'en by me.   (ll.54-55)

Then, seeing a disdainful look on her face (we must remember that this is the future "she-wolf of France"), he says, "Go, and be free again, as Suffolk's friend" (l.59). As she turns to go he stops her:

> O stay . . . I have no power to let her pass;
> My hand would free her but my heart says no.   (ll.60-61)

He is daunted by her "gorgeous beauty" and dares not speak. He thinks of calling for pen and paper and putting his love in writing, but is ashamed of his weakness. She now offers a ransom but he turns aside, muttering his perplexity and trying to find a way out of his difficulty. The difficulty is, of course, that he is already married.

> Fond man, remember that thou hast a wife;
> Then how can Margaret be thy paramour?   (ll.81-82)

He continues these asides for nine consecutive speeches, which are interspersed with her comments which express a growing puzzlement and the thought that he must be mad. Losing patience she shouts at him:

> Hear ye, Captain — are you not at leisure?   (l.97)

He has now conceived the idea of marrying her to his king, and he turns to speak directly to her. But she now speaks aside, giving him what she calls "*quid* for *quo*." He makes the offer and almost a serious and revealing gaffe:

> I'll undertake to make thee Henry's queen,
> To put a golden sceptre in thy hand
> And set a precious crown upon thy head,
> If thou wilt condescend to be my—
> *Mar.* What?
> *Suf.* His love   (ll.117-21)

He has retrieved the situation superficially, but his speech continues to reveal the confusion in his mind. When she protests her unworthiness to be Henry's wife he replies,

No, gentle madam, I unworthy am
To woo so fair a dame to be his wife
And have no portion in the choice myself.   (ll.123-25)

She is content with this ambiguous offer. Up to this point everything
is unhistorical except the fact that Suffolk is married, that he did
suggest the marriage of Henry and Margaret, and that Margaret was
impressive in beauty and personality. Hall said, "This woman excel-
led all other, as well in beautie and favor, as in wit and pollicie, and
was of stomack and corage, more like to a man, then a woman."[2]
One gets the impression that she understands what Suffolk hopes to
gain by the arrangement and there is no sign of confusion in her
mind. Her father, Reignier, quickly agrees and makes a hard bargain
which Suffolk undertakes will be accepted. As they part, Reignier
embraces Suffolk and Margaret says,

Farewell, my lord. Good wishes, praise and prayers
Shall Suffolk ever have of Margaret.   (ll.173-74)

He does not want to let her go and asks whether she has any message
for the King. She answers modestly but he presses her: "No loving
token for his majesty?" (l.181). She answers,

Yes, my good lord, a pure unspotted heart,
Never yet taint of love, I send the king.
Suf. And this withal. [*Kisses her*]
Mar. That for thyself. I will not so presume
To send such peevish token to a king. (ll.182-86)

All this is done and said in the presence of her father. They understand each other already. When Margaret and Reignier have gone
out, Suffolk soliloquizes. He wants her for himself but he is horrified
at what this may involve:

O wert thou for myself! But Suffolk, stay;
Thou mayst not wander in that labyrinth;
There minotaurs and ugly treasons lurk.   (ll.187-89)

Even if he is able to avoid the dangers, she may be Ariadne to his
Theseus, a not entirely happy story. He decides to praise her virtues
and natural graces to Henry in such a manner as will "bereave him of
his wits with wonder." We do not hear Suffolk praising Margaret to
the King, for when Act V, scene v, begins Suffolk has ended his
account of Margaret's charms and Henry is suitably impressed. He is
easily induced by Suffolk to break off his betrothal to the Earl of Arm-

agnac's daughter, in spite of the protests of Gloucester and Exeter.
Henry asks Suffolk to return at once to France to bring back Margaret. *Part I* ends with Suffolk's comment:

> Thus Suffolk hath prevail'd; and thus he goes
> As did the youthful Paris once to Greece,
> With hope to find the like event in love,
> But prosper better than the Trojan did.
> Margaret shall now be queen, and rule the king:
> But I will rule both her, the king and realm.   (V.v.103-8)

The comparison with Paris is apt, for he intends to steal a king's wife.
He realizes the dangers implied in the comparison but hopes to be
luckier in the end than Paris was. We remember the disasters brought
upon Troy by Paris's exploit, and we are prepared for similar results
in England. The last line of the soliloquy is an echo of Hall: Suffolk
"by the meanes of the Quene, was shortely erected to the estate and
degree of a Duke, and ruled the Kyng at his pleasure."[3] Again,
before dying, Suffolk will compare himself to heroes of antiquity (*2
Henry VI*, IV.i), with no sign of irony on Shakespeare's part but
rather the hint that we should take him seriously. Similarly, Margaret compares herself to Dido (III.ii.115-18), and Suffolk's farewell
speech (end of III.ii.) has echoes of the exiled Ovid's complaint to his
wife.[4] Shakespeare put this pair of lovers in famous company.

In Act I, scene iii, the Queen and Suffolk are walking in the palace grounds — clearly confirmed now in their intimacy — when they
meet some petitioners, one of whom takes Suffolk to be Gloucester,
the Lord Protector. The petitions anger both the Queen and Suffolk,
and Margaret complains about her treatment at Court. She is annoy-
ed that her husband is "a pupil still," and she compares him unfav-
ourably with Suffolk:

> I tell thee, Pole, when in the city Tours
> Thou ran'st a tilt in honour of my love,
> And stol'st away the ladies' hearts of France,
> I thought King Henry had resembled thee
> In courage, courtship and proportion;
> But all his mind is bent to holiness,
> To number Ave-Maries on his beads. . .   (ll.50-56)

Suffolk tries to content her with a promise:

> Madam, be patient: as I was the cause
> Your Highness came to England, so will I
> In England work your Grace's full content.   (ll.65-67)

Their association is partly one of political ambition, but it is important to remember that he fell in love with her before he knew who she was and certainly before he conceived the plan of marrying her to his king.

Suffolk is already setting traps for Margaret's enemies, notably the Gloucesters. The spirit's answers in the séance contrived by Suffolk are Shakespeare's inventions and the unhistorical prophecy, "By water shall he die and take his end" (I.iv.32), is remembered by Suffolk on the day of his death. In the play Margaret's great rival is Eleanor, duchess of Gloucester, and this again is unhistorical for Eleanor's humiliation took place four years before Margaret came to England. Shakespeare brought it forward so that the struggle for control of the King and of England should fall chiefly between Suffolk and Margaret on the one hand and Gloucester and his wife on the other. A brilliant invention on Shakespeare's part is the dropping of the fan by Margaret and the box she administers to Eleanor's ear in the pretence that she took her for a servant. Eleanor's answer sends shivers down one's back:

> ... proud Frenchwoman,
> Could I come near your beauty with my nails,
> I'd set my ten commandments in your face.   (I.iii.149-42)

In Act II, scene i, Suffolk, in close attendance on Henry and Margaret, feels confident enough to taunt Gloucester, and in Act III, scene i, he arrests Gloucester on a trumped-up charge of treason. Beaufort, York, and Suffolk decide on Gloucester's death in the presence of Margaret and by the next scene Gloucester is dead, strangled by Suffolk's murderers. He has been laid in a bed to counterfeit a natural death. The King knows that it is murder, but Margaret defends Suffolk and puts on an act of ill-treated martyrdom. Warwick enters to announce that the commons have heard a report that Gloucester has been murdered by Suffolk and Beaufort and that they demand to know the truth. Warwick indicates the evidence of murder in the dead Gloucester's appearance, and a shouting match between Warwick and Suffolk leads to the drawing of weapons.

At the demand of the commons, Henry banishes Suffolk. Margaret pleads for him in vain, and they are left alone on the stage to curse their enemies and bewail their coming separation. She weeps over his clutched hand and then kisses it:

> O, could this kiss be printed in thy hand,
> That thou might'st think upon these by the seal
> Through whom a thousand sighs are breath'd for thee.
>   (III.ii.342-44)

(This is the first occurrence of the seal-mouth image which runs through Shakespeare's work.) They embrace and kiss, ''Loather a hundred times to part than die'' (l.354). For Suffolk the banishment is from her, not from England:

> 'Tis not the land I care for, wert thou thence:
> A wilderness is populous enough
> So Suffolk had thy heavenly company.   (ll.358-60)

He asks her to let him stay with her, even at the risk of death:

> If I depart from thee I cannot live;
> And in thy sight to die, what were it else
> But like a pleasant slumber in thy lap?
> Here could I breathe my soul into the air,
> As mild and gentle as the cradle-babe
> Dying with mother's dug between its lips;
> Where, from thy sight, I should be raging mad,
> And cry out for thee to close up mine eyes,
> To have thee with thy lips to stop my mouth.
> So shouldst thou either turn my flying soul
> Or I should breathe it so into thy body
> And then it liv'd in sweet Elysium . . .   (ll.387-98)

But they must part; she in the hope of meeting again, he full of foreboding of death:

> *Mar.* Though parting be a fretful corrosive,
>   It is applied to a deathful wound.
>   To France, sweet Suffolk! Let me hear from thee,
>   For whereso'er thou art in this world's globe
>   I'll have an Iris that shall find thee out,
>   Away!
> *Suf.* I go.
> *Mar.* And take my heart with thee. [*She kisses him.*]
> *Suf.* A jewel lock'd into the woefull'st cask
>   That ever did contain a thing of worth.
>   Even as a splitted bark so sunder we:
>   This way fall I to death.
> *Mar.* This way for me.   (ll.402-12)

So ends Act III, scene ii. Almost immediately, in Act IV, scene i, comes Suffolk's end. In a sea battle on his way to France, Suffolk has been taken prisoner with two other gentlemen. Hall tells us that his head was struck off on the side of a cock boat; head and body were left on the shore to be picked up by Suffolk's chaplain, who took the body to Wingfield College for burial. Shakespeare's invented version is very different. According to him, the two gentlemen promise to pay for their freedom but Suffolk has been allotted to Walter Whitmore — a character unknown to history but invented by Shakespeare to carry out the similarly invented prophecy that Suffolk will die by water, Walter being pronounced as water. Whitmore has lost an eye in the affray and is determined to kill Suffolk in dogged retribution. Suffolk recognizes the Captain[6] as one who has served at Court, and he trusts that this will save him. But the proud and contemptuous way in which he reminds the Captain of his former servile state hardens the latter's heart against him. In return, the Captain bitterly and offensively recounts the memory of what he has observed at Court. He lays the losses in France, the troubles at home, and the death of Gloucester squarely at Suffolk's door. Punning on Suffolk's family name, Pole (pronounced pool), he cries out,

> Poole! Sir Poole! Lord!
> Ay, kennel, puddle, sink, whose filth and dirt[7]
> Troubles the silver spring where England drinks.
> Now will I dam up this thy yawning mouth,
> For swallowing the treature of the realm.
> Thy lips that kiss'd the Queen shall sweep the ground . . .
> (IV.i.69-74)

To Shakespeare's mind, the physical degree to which the love of Margaret and Suffolk had gone must have been common knowledge at Court. Whitmore has mockingly referred to Suffolk as the "forlorn swain" (l.65), the abandoned lover of the Queen, for that is surely the intention of this cruel joke. Suffolk at first pleads the Queen's commission, but then his pride supervenes and he decides to die bravely, without any further attempt to soften his captors:

> Come soldiers, show what cruelty you can,
> That this my death may never be forgot.
> Great men oft die by vile besonians:
> A Roman soldier and banditto slave
> Murder'd sweet Tully; Brutus' bastard hand
> Stabb'd Julius Ceasar; savage islanders
> Pompey the Great; and Suffolk dies by pirates.   (ll.132-38)

He is removed for execution and a moment later Whitmore carries
the severed head and body onto the stage, saying,

> There let his head and lifeless body lie,
> Until the Queen his mistress bury it.   (ll.142-43)

The horrified Gentleman cries out,

> O barbarous and bloody spectacle!
> His body will I bear unto the King:
> If he revenge it not, yet will his friends;
> So will the Queen, that living held him dear.   (ll.144-47)

But we are not told who took the head to the Queen. A little later, in
Act IV, scene iv, we see Margaret in King Henry's presence, holding
Suffolk's head to her breast. Grief has made her reckless in shame-
lessly acknowledging her love.

> Oft have I heard that grief softens the mind,
> And makes it fearful and degenerate;
> Think therefore on revenge, and cease to weep.
> But who can cease to weep and look on this?
> Here may his head lie on my throbbing breast,
> But where's the body that I should embrace?   (ll.1-6)

It is not long since she held the living head of her departing lover to
her breast. While the King discusses the Jack Cade rebellion with his
lords, Margaret continues her lament:

> Ah! barbarous villains, hath this lovely face
> Rul'd like a wandering planet over me,
> And could it not enforce them to relent
> That were unworthy to behold the same?   (ll.15-18)

The King turns to her:

> How now, madam?
> Still lamenting and mourning for Suffolk's death?
> I fear me, love, if that I had been dead,
> Thou wouldst not have mourn'd so much for me.

Even in this situation she is quick-witted enough to reply, with ready
and triumphant hypocrisy, "My love, I should not mourn but die for
thee" (ll.21-24). The rebels are reported to be drawing near and
Margaret says that if Suffolk were alive, "the Kentish rebels would
be soon appeased." As she goes out, still nursing the head, she
replies, "My hope is gone, now Suffolk is deceas'd" (ll.54-55).

So ends the story of Suffolk and Margaret, but there is yet
another, more oblique reference to this love in the suggestion, in *3
Henry VI* (II.ii.131 ff.), that the Prince of Wales is its fruit. The
spirited young prince stands up to Warwick:

> If that be right which Warwick says is right,
> There is no wrong, but everything is right.

Warwick comments,

> Whoever got thee, there thy mother stands.

Ten lines later Edward, soon to be Edward IV, attacks Margaret as
"shameless callet."

> Helen of Greece was fairer far than thou,
> Although thy husband may be Menelaus;
> And ne'er was Agamemnon's brother wrong'd
> By that false woman as this king by thee.

We remember Suffolk's description of himself going to France to
bring Margaret to England, "As did the youthful Paris once to
Greece" (*I Henry VI,* V.v.104). Critics and commentators appear to
have ignored the paternity of Edward, Prince of Wales, as implied by
these speeches and therefore as it appeared to Shakespeare.

This then is the tragic tale of adulterous love which Shakespeare
based upon the merest hints in history. Hall once referred to Suffolk
as "the Quenes dearlynge" and stated that the Queen "entierly
loved the Duke,"[8] but even here darling could mean favourite (there is
reference to the Queen's "minion") and the entire love is not necessarily sexual. Holinshed, whose *Chronicle* Shakespeare closely followed, omitted these hints of an affection but stressed the close association of Suffolk and Margaret in the control of the country. In
tracing the disruption of England under Henry VI, Holinshed wrote,
"Richard, duke of Yorke, ... perceiving the king to be no ruler, but
the whole burthen of the realme to rest in direction of the queene, &
the duke of Suffolke, began secretlie to allure his friends of the
nobilitie."[9] When the commons began openly to accuse Suffolk of
being the cause of the many ills afflicting England, Holinshed said,
"The queene hereat, doubting not onelie the dukes destruction, but
also hir owne confusion, caused the parlement, before begun at the
Blackfriers, to be adjourned to Leicester; thinking there, by force and
rigor of law, to suppresse and subdue all the malice and evill conceived against the duke & hir."[10] Shakespeare is justified by the

Chronicles for holding this disastrous association of Suffolk and Margaret, as much as the weakness of the King, responsible for the fearful events which the tetralogy relates. He went yet further. But for this love, to Shakespeare's mind, the French provinces would not have been lost, the good Duke of Gloucester would not have been murdered, the crown would not have passed to the house of York, and Richard, Duke of Gloucester, might never have had the opportunities for the slaughter which brought him to the throne as Richard III. When later, in *Richard III*, we watch the aging Margaret lurking in the background to observe the terrible consequences of her association with Suffolk and of her husband's holy weakness, we should remember this, her only love. It is Shakespeare's first essay in tragic, destructive love, and there is something grand in this shameless affection between two passionate, ruthless, and physically splendid lovers. That it is neither historically nor dramatically called for may be the reason why Shakespeare partly concealed it by dividing it between two plays. Of course, it does tie *Parts 1* and *2* together in the most exciting way, since we see Suffolk's statement of his intentions in the last lines of *Part I* being put into operation at the very beginning of *Part 2*. Put wholly into one play, however, this stated purpose and its carrying out could steal the show and make a mock of history. But spoken in their entirety, as they probably were in the original productions, the Suffolk-Margaret scenes would hold their own against the historical material, and the more intimate and continuous association of the lovers on the stage, even in the presence of other characters, would give flesh to Shakespeare's view of this segment of English history.

Recent productions of *Henry VI*, concentrating on the Wars of the Roses rather than on the human interest and relationships of Shakespeare's play and making the weakness of the King and the ruthless covetousness of the barons the cause of all, have cut the three great scenes — the courtship, the farewell, and the death of Suffolk — so that the love story almost disappears from the play and the nursing of Suffolk's severed head by Margaret almost becomes a shocking irrelevance. Critics and commentators too have played it down, embarrassed perhaps that a queen of England should have behaved thus and that Shakespeare should have invented such a tasteless story. Other meaningless excisions in recent productions — the omission of the Countess-Talbot and Pucelle-Burgundy scenes in *I Henry VI* at Stratford — have robbed that play of passages of high and complex human interest and made such productions heavy with history, shorn of those parts of these plays which perhaps most interested their author, partly because he invented them.

Suffolk's brave death and the effects his deeds had, in Shakespeare's view, on English history, raise him to tragic level. His comparison of his own death with those of Tully, Julius Caesar, and Pompey is not there to be laughed at; neither is his own likening of himself to Paris and of Margaret to Helen, nor the associations with Dido and Aeneas and Ovid and his wife. And one is inevitably reminded of Lancelot and Guinevere. [11] The disastrous consequences of this love were made by Shakespeare to seem similar to those of the other adulterous love upon Troy, which Shakespeare was to set forth in *Troilus and Cressida.* It is a love as splendidly physical but as morally and politically reprehensible as that of Antony and Cleopatra, while Margaret in her ferocity is an earlier Lady Macbeth. For Margaret, Suffolk is the only love, the rest is bitterness. For Suffolk, the world was well lost in her service and its memory enables him to die nobly and proudly. Margaret's nursing of the hewn-off head is a tribute unique in love stories. His loss and the fuller realization of the unheroic qualities of her husband turn her into the doomed and desperate warrior queen, not to be released by death but to live on into *Richard III* — a malevolent ghost haunting Richard, commenting on the fateful developments, and cursing her enemies. The attitude of conventional morality to this love is expressed not in Henry's peevish comments but in the Lieutenant's condemnation, [12] and here the rough English view triumphs in dooming Suffolk unceremoniously to death. So respectable Romans must have thought of Antony and Cleopatra. But Margaret's exit with the head could be almost as strange and awe-inspiring as the madness of Lady Macbeth if the full text were performed to sustain it.

The historical part of the Suffolk story, as it was presented by the Tudor historians, [13] was sufficiently well known to be used as a moral example in *A Myrroure for Magistrates* (1559), ''How Lorde William Delapole Duke of Suffolke was worthily punyshed for abusing his Kyng and causing the destruction of good Duke Humfrey.'' But there is no mention of love here either. How effective Shakespeare's distortions of and additions to history were may be judged from Drayton's *Englands Heroicall Epistles* (1598). Drayton pretended to depend upon ''Chronicle Historie'' in compiling these imaginary verse letters between famous English lovers, and on the title page he directed his readers to observe his pertinent annotations. But he had only Shakespeare's authority for a famous love betwen Queen

Margaret and Suffolk, and much of what Drayton gave as historical fact is Shakespearean invention. In the Epistle from "Elinor Cobham to Duke Humphrey," we are told, "Poole needs must have his Darling made a Queene" (l.80).[14] (Does the use of the word darling here suggest that Drayton too had read Hall before writing these Epistles?) "The Argument" of the exchange of letters between Suffolk and Margaret begins:

> This Duke of Suffolke, William, to advance
> A Lady, long belov'd of him in France,
> His Mistris, Margaret, that Duke Rayners Child,
> Himselfe who of Jerusalem instyl'd
> The King: this Poole, his Darling to preferre,
> Betwixt young Henry, nam'd the sixt, and her,
> Concludes a Marriage ...   (p.230)

Margaret's letter is written after Suffolk's banishment, and she expresses her sense of personal and political deprivation. She warns Suffolk of the dangers of the sea:

> I pray thee, Poole, have care how thou do'st passe,
> Never the Sea yet halfe so dang'rous was;
> And one fore-told, by Water thou should'st die ...
>   (p.242; ll.139-41)

Drayton solemnly annotated this as though it came from the Chronicles. "The Witch of Eye received answere from her Spirit, That the Duke of Suffolke should take heed of Water: Which the Queene fore-warnes him of, as remembring the Witches Prophesie; which afterwards came to passe" (p.246). We know, of course, that Shakespeare was the only source of this prophecy.

But if the Chronicles are silent, apart from the merest hints, in the matter of the love of Margaret and Suffolk, there is another source to suggest an authentic love affair between them. Suffolk has been revealed as a courtly poet, and poems previously attributed to Charles D'Orléans are now generally accepted as by Suffolk.[15] One of these at least, "Praise of a Flower," is taken as having been addressed to Queen Margaret (Marguerite). It begins,

> Myn hert ys set, and all myn hole entent,
>   To serve this flour in my most humble wyse
> As faythfully as can be thought or ment,
>   Wyth-out feynyng or slouthe in my servyse;
>   For wytt the wele, yt ys a paradyse
>   To se this floure when yt begyn to sprede,
>   Wyth colours fressh ennewyd, white and rede.[16]

Another poem is a conventional complaint against fortune, but yet another (p.189) is entitled "Lettyr" and begins,

> Myn hertys Ioy, and all myn hole plesaunce,
> Whom that I serve and shall do faythfully.

In spite of the "wyth-out feynyng," "Praise of a Flower" might be dismissed as a courtly exercise in the manner of medieval gallantry, but this last little poem has a ring of sincerity which might well have come from Suffolk's banishment:

> I wryte to yow no more for lak of space,
>   But i beseche the only trinite
> Yow kepe and save be support of hys grace,
>   And be your sheld from all adversyte.
>   Go lytill byll, and say thou were wyth me
>   Of verey trouth, as thou canst wele remembre,
>   At myn upryst, the fyft day of Decembre. [17]

Had Drayton actually seen any of Suffolk's poems? I almost think he had when I read in Margaret's Epistle,

> My Daisie flower, which erst perfum'd the ayre,
> Which for my favour Princes dayn'd to weare . . .   (p.241; ll.89-90)

But the play on Daisy-Marguerite-Margaret is perhaps too obvious to require knowledge of Suffolk's poem. Drayton noted, "The Daisie in French is called Margarite, which was Queene Margarets Badge; wherewithall the Nobilitie and Chivalrie of the Land, at her first Arrivall, were so delighted, that they wore it in their Hats, in token of Honour" (pp.244-45).

It may be equally idle to speculate whether Shakespeare might have read or heard of Suffolk's poems for, even if he had, this would not lessen the range and significance of his inventions in setting forth this story and in linking it with the struggle for power. In Suffolk and Margaret, Shakespeare was already reaching out toward his great tragic relationships, not with full confidence yet but with astonishing boldness for an early play with which he was hoping to establish himself in the world of the theatre. And he did this with more poetry, insight, and power than his *Henry VI* is usually credited with.

---

[1] *The first Part of King Henry VI*, Arden edition, ed. A.S. Cairncross (London, 1962). All quotations are from this edition unless otherwise noted.

[2] Edward Hall, *The Union of the Two Noble and Illustre Famelies of Lancastre and Yorke* (London, 1550), fol. cxlviii^v.

[3] Hall, fol. cxlix-cl. The last line of Suffolk's speech resembles the younger Mortimer's plea to Queen Isabella in Marlowe's *Edward II*, "Be ruled by me, and we will rule the realme . . ." (*Edward II*, V.ii.5, ed. W.M. Merchant, New Mermaid, Benn, London, 1967, l. 2147). But both these lines are traceable to the Chronicles, and the relationship between Queen Isabella and Mortimer is similar to that between Margaret and Suffolk. Both women become warrior queens; Isabella before, Margaret after her lover's death. Mortimer's severed head is brought onto the stage, but immediately after Isabella's exit at the end of the play. Shakespeare went much further in intensifying the passion between the lovers and in the invention of the prolonged farewell and the pathetic and grotesque hugging of Suffolk's head by Margaret. The adulterous affair is more dramatically justifiable but less interesting in Marlowe's play than in Shakespeare's, but the question of influence awaits agreement on the relative dating of the two plays.

[4] *The Second Part of King Henry VI*, Arden edition, ed. A.S. Cairncross (London, 1957), p. 96. Further quotations from the play are from this edition unless otherwise noted.

[5] Hall, fol. cxlviii.

[6] Referred to as "Lieutenant" in FF.

[7] There have been several attempts to clear up some confusion in these two lines. This is substantially the First Folio version. For others, see Arden edition, ed. Cairncross, p. 104.

[8] Hail, fol. clviii.

[9] Raphael Holinshed, . . . *The Chronicles of England, Scotlande, and Irelande* (London, 1587), III,627.

[10] Holinshed, III,631.

[11] Arden edition, ed. Cairncross, p. liv.

[12] IV.i.69-102.

[13] Modern historians have found him a worthier person.

[14] Michael Drayton, *Works*, ed. William Hebel (Oxford, 1931-41), II, 217. All quotations are taken from this edition.

[15] See H.N. MacCracken, "An English Friend of Charles of Orléans," *PMLA*, XXVI, new ser., XIX (1911), 142-80.

[16] Quotations from R.H. Robbins, *Secular Lyrics of the XIVth and XVth Centuries* (Oxford, 1952), p. 186.

[17] Robbins, p. 190.

Welshmen in Shakespeare's Stratford

For some six centuries, whenever they have been allowed to do so, Welshmen have descended from their bleak hills to better themselves financially amongst their neighbours to the east, and Warwickshire, a prosperous and pleasant county on the road to Barnet and London, has throughout these centuries been one of their main settling places.

During the early fifteenth century, as a result of Owain Glyndŵr's unsuccessful bid for freedom, discriminatory statutes had been passed against Welshmen. In 1400-1 it was ordained that "none of them be received to any office of Mayor, Bailiff, Chamberlain, Constable, or Keeper of the Gate, or of the Gaol."[1] This referred specifically to border towns or merchant towns adjacent to the Marches, but it must be remembered that Stratford and Alcester were less than ten miles from the boundary of the Marches. Another clause in this same statute orders that no Welshman is to purchase land or tenements in England, nor to be accepted burgess, nor to have any liberty within the realm.[2] And all statutes against Welshmen were confirmed by the only Act of the Parliament of 1446-7 (25 Henry VI).

In the sixteenth century, with the Act of Union to legalize them,[3] the Welsh came to Warwickshire in considerable numbers, and such names as Ap Rice, ap Gryffen, ap Lewis and Gwillim are to be found in the Alcester parish register during the reigns of Elizabeth and James I.[4] A Welsh element is also conspicuous at the same time at Salford Priors, Wellesbourne, Hampton Lucy, and Tamworth.[5] The same, as we shall see, was true of Stratford-upon-Avon. During the seventeenth century Welsh names became anglicized and the Welsh disappeared into the communities amongst which they had settled. The registers of marriage show that Welshmen usually married English girls and this no doubt helped in the process, but even today a paper like the *Leamington Courier* will afford striking evidence of the persistence of some of the sixteenth century Welsh names.

I propose to limit my search for Welsh men and women at Stratford to a period of about forty-seven years, from the date of the proclamation of the town as a royal borough in 1553 to the end of the century, that is, two years after the death of the most notable Stratford Welshman, Lewis ap Williams.

Most of the Welshmen who lived at Stratford or who sojourned there in Shakespeare's day were of humble station, and only two of them filled offices under the Corporation. A third, though not a Stratford man, was headmaster of the grammar school during Shakespeare's formative years. Some were shopkeepers, an ironmonger and a butcher, others were craftsmen, one a dependable armourer and cutler, another a tinker and brass-worker. One, perhaps not a resident, was a rabbit-dealer, and one is left anonymous and disreputable. ''The Twelve men do present that the Welsheman using to archarey in Shypstret[6] lyvethe Idly and Suspecyously.''[7] Idly and suspiciously, a serious accusation in busy Stratford and not one that could be levelled at most other Welshmen there in the sixteenth century. Let us begin with the most industrious of them, Lewis ap Williams, for long years alderman and, in his turn, bailiff (we would today say mayor) of Stratford-upon-Avon.

Lewis ap Williams

Lewis ap Williams[8] was an ironmonger who lived in the High Street. The one unfortunate association of his name with the sale of unwholesome fish[9] need not justify his being called a fishmonger as well. Like all Stratford Welshmen, his origin is unknown,[10] but he was already sufficiently well established and well thought of in the town to be sworn in as one of the twelve members of the jury at the first court leet, 6 April 1554,[11] to be held under the newly incorporated borough of Stratford. An even greater sign of early trust was his selection on that occasion as one of the four affeerors, for the duty of an affeeror was to decide upon the amount a person was to be fined for an infringement of the borough regulations.

At this meeting new by-laws were passed, but it is clear that their purpose was to strengthen established traditions in the running of the town. The burgesses confirmed the freedom of Stratford for all comers and their wares ''as they have done in tymes past.'' Regulations were passed against the allowing of unmuzzled dogs in the streets, against the uncontrolled depositing of garbage, and against the reception into any house within the borough of any strange women with child.[12]

Lewis ap Williams is present again as a juror at the view of frankpledge[13] of 4 October 1554, and again on 26 April 1555. On 11 October 1555 he is ordained constable,[14] together with William Smyth, who was most likely Shakespeare's godfather. The office of constable was, as we shall see later, an arduous and sometimes even dangerous one. The *Book of Orders* of 1557,[15] in detailing the duties of constables, requires that the four constables, upon pain to forfeit six shillings and eightpence apiece to the bailiff and burgesses of the borough of Stratford, shall call unto them a convenient number of the company once every month to keep a privy watch for the good government of the town. The records show that the constables, in visiting ale-houses or tracking down gaming tables, often ran into trouble and even lost blood.[16]

Lewis ap Williams is present at the view of frankpledge of 7 April 1556 and again on 2 October 1556. He is not summoned to act on the jury for the view of frankpledge meeting of 30 April 1557, for he himself is concerned in a matter which comes up before it, concerning a house in High Street. It is reported in Latin.[17] With Lewis ap Williams present and listed as capital burgess,[18] the council on 29 September 1557 drew up the *Book of Orders* to which I have already referred. This for the first time in the life of the borough regulated procedure, the election of officers, the meetings of hall in the council chamber, and the holding of courts leet twice a year. It stressed the necessity for secrecy and brotherly love amongst the members of the council and required the bailiff, aldermen, and capital burgesses to hang a lanthorn with a candle burning in it before their doors from 15 December until the twentieth day after Christmas. So Lewis ap Williams's house in High Street must have been distinguished by a lighted lantern in the unlit Stratford streets during the Christmas season from now on.

At the view of frankpledge of 1 October 1557[19] Lewis ap Williams is again affeeror, with John Taylor, and at this same meeting he is elected to the important post of chamberlain, together with Roger Sadler. The chamberlains handled the finances of the corporation, and election to this post implied honesty, skill in the handling of money, and the ability to read and write. At this meeting too Thomas Dycson is fined three shillings and fourpence for "drawynge blud" in a quarrel with Lewes ap William. This is probably a result of the latter's activity as constable or as a member of the watch, for this Dycson, *alias* waterman of the Swan, was a questionable character and was twice fined in the year 1560-1 for suffering unlawful gaming.

At the view of frankpledge of 23 April 1558,[20] though Lewis ap Williams is once more down as affeeror, he himself stands amerced, i.e. fined, for digging gravel in Tinkers Street.[21] On 29 September 1558, together with Roger Sadler, he presents the first known chamberlains' account to the Stratford council. This account ends:

> The Chamberlains are in debt to the Chamber ten shillings which remaineth in the hands of the said Lews ap Wylliam unto the next account.

At the view of frankpledge on the following day he is again elected chamberlain for the coming year, this time with Richard Hill.[22] At a meeting of 14 April 1559 he is present as Lodowycus ap Wyllyam and is once again affeeror. So also on 6 October 1559,[23] when the minutes give us our first specimen of the mark or sign of Lewis ap Williams. This has been said to resemble a church gable and to mean Holy Church. That the reader may judge for himself, here is a representation of it.[24]

It may be as well to deal immediately with all the occurrences of this mark to be seen in the minutes. In May 1561 slight differences are to be observed, the drawing is rather uncertain but the cross is clearer.[15]

On 27 September 1564 the mark is again boldly drawn and is the most conspicuous mark on the page.[26]

Thirty years after its first occurrence, on 29 January 1588-9, it has been greatly simplified and is now done sweepingly across the page.[27]

It was not often that decisions taken at hall were of sufficient moment to require signatures. On these occasions John Shakespeare drew an elegant pair of glover's dividers, the symbol of his guild. In neither case, that of Lewis ap Williams or the poet's father, does the use of a sign mean or suggest illiteracy. Such marks were commonly used in the sixteenth century, particularly by guild members and craftsmen, even when they wrote quite well. And both these signs are very far removed from the roughly drawn cross which we associate with the hand unfamiliar with pen and ink.

At the view of frankpledge of 5 October 1560, Lewis ap Williams is once more affeeror, but the following item appears in the list of infringements of the borough regulations:

> Edward Yngram, Lews ap William, Robert Hynd, for syllynge fysh sumtyme not holsum they stand a merced.[28]

Most of the notable townsmen of Stratford were caught at some time or other infringing the regulations of the town, some of them even during the year of their bailiwick, but Lewis ap Williams was never in serious trouble. During these early years he took cases for the recovery of small sums of money against several people and the Court of Record MSS list actions taken by him against William Mors, in 1554, over some madder and alum he had sold him, against Elizabeth Marten for debt in 1556, against Francis Torpley in 1561, and again against Edmund Myculton.

On 4 May 1561, John Shakespeare joins Lewis ap Williams as affeeror to the court.[29] On this day a large number of townsmen were fined, including the bailiff, Roger Sadler, who was involved in two separate infringements. On 26 January 1563-4 a memorandum in the council minutes states:

> At a Hall ther holden ye XXVIt day of Januarye anno predicto the Chambur ys ffound in arerage and in dept unto Lewes ap William XXVIs vijd.
> Item at ye same hall the Chamber is found in arerage and ys in det unto John Shakespeyr xxvjs vijd.[30]

On 30 August 1564 Lewis ap Williams contributes two shillings towards the relief of the poor, and on 27 September twelve pence more.[31] On these occasions John Shakespeare's contribution was exactly half that of his Welsh colleague. The reason for this repeated and considerable call upon the charity of the wealthier members of the community was the terrible plague which descended upon Stratford in the summer of 1564, a plague thought to have been brought from Havre by the Earl of Warwick's soldiers. On 11 July John Bretchgirdle, the vicar, had written *hic incepit pestis* in the parish register of burials, and from July to December the lists of the buried are pitifully long.

Lewis ap Williams was absent from the hall of 6 September 1564, but his absence is excused, which means that he showed good reason for it, and in the minutes of this meeting he is listed as an alderman. From now on he attends regularly once more. The meeting of 27 September was an important occasion, one of those on which the members of the council appended their signatures and marks to the decisions taken. John Wheler had been chosen bailiff but was reluctant to take up this costly and onerous office at a time when the plague was raging. The council sternly orders him to take up his duties, but the fact that Richard Hill is shown as bailiff in December shows that Wheler successfully resisted. By 20 October[32] Lewis ap Williams has become Mr Alderman, that is chief alderman and J.P. The other Justice of the Peace was always the bailiff. His rapid rise shows the esteem in which he must have been held. At the meeting of 20 December 1564 he is again Mr Alderman, a position he holds for the following year. On the previous day, 19 December, the register of baptisms records the baptizing of his son Lewis, given as Lodovicus filius Lodovici Apwilliams. He is present at hall on 15 February and again on 21 March 1564-5[33] for the presentation of the chamberlains' account for the preceding year. Considerable sums of money have been paid to him during this year, no doubt for him to pay on behalf of the council in his capacity as chief alderman.

```
pd to Mr Lewes . . . . . . . . . . . . . . . . . . . . . . . . . . . . . . xxvjs viijd
pd to Mr Lews for Ric Sharpe[34] . . . . . . . . . . . . . . . . . . . . . . xxxs
pd to Mr Lews . . . . . . . . . . . . . . . . . . . . . . . . . . . . . . . . xvijs
```

At this same meeting a quittance is made for two former chamberlains, Richard Hill and Lewis ap Williams.[35] This means that they have handed over any money which came into their charge during their year of office.

Lewis ap Williams attends hall on the following day and twice during May 1565. At the hall of 9 May[36] he is involved in the expulsion from the council of William Bot for using evil words of the council. At the same meeting Lewis ap Williams and Adrian Quyny are deputed ''to make labour and make suit to the Earl of Warwick for the obtaining of such liberties as the said Lord of Warwick hath within the borough of Stratford and they to be recompensed for their pains so to be taken.'' From later payments, however, it appears that John Wheler made up for his earlier defection by taking Lewis ap Williams's place in this matter. On 4 July 1565 Lewis ap Williams is present at hall when John Shakespeare is elected alderman.[37] He attends each recorded hall for the next two years and in 1567-8[39] the sum of sixteen shillings is recorded as having been paid to him for the Queen's carriage. This sum represented the Stratford share of the cost of the Queen's progress from Warwick to Woodstock via Charlecote.

On 18 August 1568 a son is born to him but is hurriedly baptized at home and dies.[40] On 4 September he is present at hall for the electing of John Shakespeare as bailiff of Stratford-upon-Avon. The chamberlains' account for 26 January 1568-9 record a payment to him of eighteenpence for a lock and a pair of hinges. In 1569 Johannes Shakyspeare and Lewes ap Wyllyams are called upon to arbitrate in a case for the Court of Record.[41] In 1570, 1571, and 1572 his attendance at hall is regular, except for 6 September 1570 and 18 April 1572, when his absence is pardoned. In April another son is born to him and baptized as Philip filius Lewis ap Williams. On 5 September 1571[42] he is nominated for the bailiwick, together with Roger Sadler and Adrian Quyny, but Quyny is elected. On 20 June 1572 he goes to Warwick with George Whately and John Shakespeare to attend the inquest on Thomas Badger.[43]

At the hall of 9 September 1573 the great moment comes when Lewis ap Williams is elected bailiff of Stratford. At the very first meeting of the council under his bailiwick an interesting order is passed concerning drovers:

> Yt is fyrther ordeyned that no drover or other foriner shall suffer their beastes or sheppe to continew and pasture in and upon Bancrofte[44] above the space of one howre upon payne of forfeiture for every time that any shall offend contrary to this ordinance 6d to be levyed upon his goodes and cattells to the use of the chamber.
>
> Yt is further ordeyned that Mr baylyf for time beinge shall nominate and appointe somme convenient personne to pynne all horses, geldings, mares, swyne, geses, duckes and other cattell going in Bancrofte or elsewhere within the precinct of this boroughe contrary to any ordinaunce heretofore made.[45]

It is curious that the first Welshman to be bailiff of Stratford-upon-Avon should have been so outstandingly concerned in the

restriction of activities in which his fellow-countrymen, as many of
these "drovers or foriners" must have been, were involved, but one
may well imagine this good and diligent burgess putting his adopted
town first and any national considerations second. And as a shopkeeper he probably thought drovers a rough and dubious set of rascals
anyhow.

The chamberlains' account for 17 February 1573-4[46] records
several payments to Lewis ap Williams sometimes by name and
sometimes as bailiff:

pd Mr Lewes for Mr Vicars tenthe[47] . . . . xxjs viiid
pd Mr Bayly for nails about the schoolfloor . . . . ijs ijd
pd Mr Bayly for lathes & lathe nails . . . . vd
pd Mr Lewes for a hundred & a half of nails . . . . xjd
pd Mr Lewes for nails . . . . iiijd
pd to Mr Bayly for the Earl of Leicester's players[48] . . . . vs viijd

These six items in themselves give some notion of his activities on his
own behalf and on behalf of the council during these busy years.
Other goods he supplied to the council are lime, at fivepence a strike,
a chain and lock to tie ladders[49] in the chapel yard,[50] fifteen fathoms
of small cord to hang the plummet of the clock at the chapel, and locks
for several purposes.

The minutes of the council meeting of 3 November 1574 are in a
strange hand and the spellings throughout are unusual. It is almost
certain, therefore, that Lewis ap Williams is the Mr Robert Lewes
whose presence is recorded.[51]

On 4 January 1574-5 the bailiff for the time being, Humphrey
Plymley, led a deputation of Stratford men to Warwick to take
delivery of the Stratford share of Thomas Oken's bequest. In the
bailiff's company went four aldermen, Adrian Quyny, Lewis ap
Williams, Richard Hill, and William Tyler, two capital burgesses,
the town clerk, and the sergeant at mace. A cheerful company they
must have made, riding along to Warwick on that winter's morning.
Thomas Oken had left one hundred and twenty pounds to be divided
equally between Warwick, Stratford and Banbury. According to the
very strict terms of his will, each forty pounds was to be divided into
eight sums of five pounds to be lent for four years to "dyvers younge
occupiers . . . that be of some honest mystery or crafte and house-
holders within the same towne."[52] Part of the interest charged on the
loan of this money was to go to the poor and part to pay for an annual
sermon with food and drink afterwards for the council. Old Oken had

been very careful in his instructions and the Stratford men were required to sign and seal a bond, pledging themselves to observe the terms of the will, before receiving the money. They thought this to be an imputation upon their business integrity and they protested, but the forceful and reasonable arguments of the bailiff of Warwick prevailed and we are told that "in thend they agreid, and the books were sealid & deliverid and the mony paid, and they of Stretford sent mery homewards."[53]

On 7 October 1575 Lewis ap Williams is present at an important hall at which the prices of ale and bread are controlled. In the chamberlains' account of 14 March 1575-6[54] payments are recorded to him for nine strikes of lime, thirteen pence worth of nails, and twopence for bringing a fire hook from Tiddington.[55] His absence from the meeting of 5 September 1576 is excused.[56] This, it is interesting to note, was John Shakespeare's last recorded hall. At the hall of 5 October 1576 Lewis ap Williams is once more chief alderman and therefore Justice of Peace. In this capacity it is his duty to entertain noble visitors to the town, and the chamberlains' account for 29 January 1577-8[57] records the payment of three shillings and eightpence to Mr Lewes for wine, ginger and lemons[58] when Lord Chandos came to Stratford. At the same time he was paid tenpence for two locks for the "gaylox," probably the gaol.

The summer of 1578 seems to have been a bad time for Stratford, possibly due to a lesser visitation of plague, for at a council meeting in November[59] it was decided that every alderman should be taxed fourpence weekly towards the relief of the poor, all except John Shakespeare and Robert Bratt, who pay nothing, and Lewis ap Williams and Humphrey Plymley, who pay threepence each. If this indicates that Lewis ap Williams was not amongst the very richest of Stratford men, at least no such slump had occurred in his affairs as is suggested in the case of the poet's father. In 1580 our alderman appears as Lewis ap Williames in the *Booke of the names and dwelling places of the Gentlemen and freeholders in the countye of Warwick.*[60]

An interesting series of entries in the chamberlains' account for 31 January 1581-2[61] affords us a glimpse of another pleasant day when civic duty went hand in hand with good living:

pd more for a pottell of sack, a pottell of claret wine and half
   a pound of sugur given to Sir John Hubande at the College[62] iijs ijd
pd to the keeper for his fee for the buck . . . . vs
pd for the dinner at the eating of the buck at Mr Lewes . . . . . . xxvjs vjd
pd for wine at the same dinner . . . . xjs xjd[63]

This is the first indication we get that Lewis ap Williams kept the sort of house at which such a feast could be put on, for it is to be noted that he was not bailiff during this year. His house was chosen because of its suitability, not on account of any official position he might hold. Sir John Hubande must have provided the buck and his game-keeper is generously tipped for bringing it to Lewis ap Williams's house. The cooking and serving of a whole buck and the serving of such a quantity of wine called not only for a capacious and well-equipped house but a knowledge of how these things are best done on the part of the master and mistress of the house. And what a dinner it must have been, for the accessories to the buck to have cost twenty-six shillings, without the wine, the equivalent to fifty pounds and more in today's money!

We will notice evidence later that Joan, wife to Lewis ap Williams, was a person of some consequence, but it is surely not too fanciful here to recognize a picture of such a feast and of her behaviour at it in Shakespeare's *Winter's Tale*, a play which has many memories of Stratford:

> When my old wife lived, upon
> This day she was both pantler, butler, cook;
> Both dame and servant; welcomed all, served all;
> Would sing her song and dance her turn, now here,
> At upper end o' the table, now i' the middle;
> On his shoulder and his; her face o fire
> With labour and the thing she took to quench it. [64]

At the hall of 13 March 1582-3,[65] Lewis ap Williams, though he is not given as present, is chosen with Adrian Quyny to collect money from the High Street ward of the town for the repair of the church. On 4 September 1583 he is nominated for bailiff, but George Whateley is elected.[66] He is sufficiently trusted to act as banker to the council and is given the sum of ten pounds to hold for it. The entry in the minutes says:[67]

> At this Hall Mr Hill did pay x li xs[68] to the use of the baylyf and burgesses of the borough aforesaid which x li was delivered to Mr Lewes to be repaid within a months warning when it shall be required.

In the autumn of 1584[69] he is once more nominated for bailiff, but this time Richard Hill is elected. The chamberlains' account for January 1585-6 shows a payment for a quantity of nails made to one Robarte Lewes. We remember that in 1574 Lewis ap Williams had been listed as Robert Lewes and that the Robert Lewes mentioned as a householder in the charter of 1553 is quite probably our man. This confusion therefore does not surprise us. There is, however, in the register of baptisms an entry for 26 March 1562:

> Robertus filius Roberti Apwilliams bapt. [70]

It is possible that Lewis ap Williams took a nephew into his business and that this payment was made to him. During the winter of 1586-7 the minutes show a number of unexcused absences from hall on Lewis ap Williams's part, suggesting illness.

The Oken's feast of 1586 was held at the house of Lewis ap Williams, though he was not bailiff, and the chamberlains' account of 13 January 1586-7 [71] records the payment of ten shillings to him for the preparation of the feast. The resources of his house are now well known and regularly called upon. In 1587 he received through the council the sum of twenty shillings for a house leased to Mary Bott in Middle Row, facing Henley Street. [72]

At hall on 6 September 1588 [73] he is once again nominated for election as bailiff but is once more disappointed, in favour of William Wilson. [74] By this time he would no doubt be pleased to see younger men filling the arduous offices of the borough. He was present at hall on 29 January 1588-9 [75] and signed the decisions of that day with the bold and simplified version of his mark which has been reproduced above. Council meetings have now become much more frequent, often twice a month, and Lewis ap Williams keeps up a good average of attendance.

The chamberlains' account of 15 January 1590-1 shows a payment of twelve shillings to Mistress Lewes for Mr Oken's feast. It is most unusual, indeed unique, that such a payment should be made and recorded to a woman, and though it may be dangerous to make too much of this point, it surely indicates that Joan Lewis was in complete charge of the economy of the household, even to the degree of being in direct contact with the council in such matters. One senses the degree to which she was responsible for Lewis ap Williams's house becoming the natural centre for the oustanding social occasions of the year in Stratford.

Lewis ap Williams must have been ill during the winter and spring, 1592-3, for between late December and early June he misses six halls in succession. He is now at least sixty-five years of age and may have given up his business, for the chamberlains' accounts now record payments for ironmongery to other men. At the hall of 19 Sep-

tember 1593[76] signatures are appended to the decisions of the day
and the names of council members, including Lewis ap Williams,
who on important occasions employ their sign, are here written out in
full. Tempting though it be to look for an actual signature here,
examination of the writing of Lewis ap Williams's name shows it to
be in a hand similar to that in which several other names, though not
all, are written. It was probably therefore that of the clerk.

There were fewer council meetings in 1594 and Lewis ap Williams attended them all except one. On 21 February 1595[77] he was
present when Margaret Griffin, widow of Griffin ap Roberts, whom
we shall look at later, brought in the five pounds her husband had
borrowed of the Oken's money. His last recorded attendance at hall
was on 22 September 1595, and when on 9 January 1596 a document
calls for signatures and marks, the distinctive gable of Lewis ap Williams is not there and the page is the emptier for it.[78] His wife died in
the summer of 1596 and the register of burials records: "June 15 Jone
wife to Mr. Lewis Williams buried."

His own long illness is recognized by the entry of the word *infir-
mus* opposite his name in the list of aldermen in the minutes of the
meetings of 20 and 27 July 1596.[79] This indication is rare in the
minutes and must show unusual concern about the health of this old,
diligent, and honoured member of the council.

With his wife dead and he himself ill and old, his house was no
longer available for Oken's feasts and other occasions of good eating
and drinking, and at the council meeting of 23 September 1597[80] it
was decided that the Oken sermon should henceforward be delivered
on election day (usually in September) and that the drinking after
should take place at the house of the bailiff for the time being.

During his long absence the name of Lewis ap Williams seems to
become unfamiliar, and on 30 November 1597 he occurs in the
minutes as Loddoig Lewes.[81] He died early in 1598 and the burial
register records: "February 8 Mr. Lewis Apwilliams buried." On
the same day his name is still included in the list of aldermen in the
minutes, though not of course marked present, so customary has it
become over the long years to see it there. At the next meeting of the
council, 15 May 1598,[82] the careless and forgetful clerk in copying
out the list once more begins to write his name. He gets as far as
Lodovicus ap — and then crosses it out. A touching end to the career
of one who was perhaps Stratford's most respected alderman during
Shakespeare's lifetime. His unwearying devotion to the town of his
adoption was at least as great as that of Adrian Quyny, whose for-

bears for many generations had lived in Stratford and held high office there.

In the vigorous young days of his career and of the life of Stratford as a borough he had sworn ''to maintain and defend the liberties and rights of the town, to the uttermost of his wit, to assist the bailiff in giving his best advice as well 'for the benefit of the town as for the good government of the same, to observe the orders, laws, and statutes, and not to disclose the speeches used by any man in the Counsel chamber concerning the affairs of the Borough.''

We may be sure that no one kept this oath more strictly than Lewis ap Williams.

Griffin ap Roberts

Another Welsh tradesman of sixteenth century Stratford was Griffin ap Roberts, the butcher, who was neither as successful, as law-abiding, nor as respected as Lewis ap Williams. His main claim to recent fame lies in the interpretation of a passage in John Aubrey's notes on Shakespeare:

> There was at that time another butcher's son in this Towne that was held not at all inferior to him for a naturall witt, his acquaintance and coetanean, but dyed young. [83]

F.J. Harries in his *Shakespeare and the Welsh* (Unwin, 1919) says that according to Aubrey, Shakespeare had as a boy a warm affection for Griffin ap Roberts, the son of a butcher, but Aubrey does not mention any name, and Griffin was the butcher, not the son. Even so it is still possible that Griffin ap Roberts was the father of this early friend of the poet. Let us consider the children allotted to Griffin ap Roberts in the Stratford registers of baptisms and burials. It will be convenient to make a list of them at this point.

John	died March 1558	
Henry	baptized March 1560-1	
	died December 1561	
John	baptized March 1562-3	
	died November 1564	
Arthur	baptized —— 1564	
	died October 1564	
Anna	baptized August 1565	
	died March 1567	
Nicholas	baptized April 1568	
	died June 1580	

William   baptized September 1571
Thomas   baptized March 1572[84]
Margret   baptized April 1568[85]

The only one of these who in any way qualifies as the boy mentioned by Aubrey is Nicholas, who died at the age of 12, when Shakespeare was 16 years old, so that he is four years out of being "coetanean." But friendship between a boy of 14 and one of 10, if they are both of unusual intelligence, is not impossible in a small town where opportunity for such friendship is limited. It is unlucky that Nicholas, having survived the first two years which were fatal to most of the Griffin ap Roberts children, should not have lived to manhood.

The first occurrences of the name of Griffin ap Roberts in the Stratford records are all connected with some breach of the borough regulations. At the view of frankpledge of 4 October 1554 he is fined fourpence for "dogges going at large and not moseled."[86] Again on 14 April 1559 he is fined twopence for a dog going at large in the street.[87] That he did not take kindly to such interference with his liberty and that of his dogs is shown by another entry that Griffin the butcher stands amerced twopence for making assault and giving opprobrious words to the constables.[88] And again he is fined fourpence for making affray upon Francis Harbadge's man.[89]

More serious still is his association with other "commen bochares and killing and syllynge flesh un wholsom." For this he was fined twelvepence on 6 October 1559.[90]

He is again in trouble, 6 May 1561, for leaving muck in Swine Street, but this time he is in good company, for the starting of unauthorized muckhills in the streets was one of the failings of some of the best Stratford men. John Shakespeare and Adrian Quyny had both been caught doing this, and at this meeting the bailiff himself, Roger Sadler, was fined on two counts.[91]

We have already seen that the plague year of 1564 hit Stratford very hard and reference to the list of his children will show that Griffin ap Roberts lost two sons, John and Arthur, in the autumn of this year, when the plague was at its height. During the years 1563 and 1564 Griffin ap Roberts had some trouble in collecting money owed to him, and the Court of Record issued the following writs and orders:

> Precept to bind over William Whateley to answer Griffin ap Roberts.[92]
> William Whateley to answer Griffin ap Roberts respecting the purchase of beef, mutton, and veal.[93]

He experienced even greater difficulty with Henry Rogers, and we do not know whether he ever got his money. A writ of capias was issued in 1564 against Henry Rogers in the matter of a debt of forty-seven shillings and eightpence and costs to Griffin ap Roberts.[94] Henry Rogers was later required to answer ap Roberts. Since there was no response from the debtor, the court issued an order to levy upon the goods of Henry Rogers,[95] and in order that this might be enforced a writ was issued to take the body of Henry Rogers to satisfy the debt.[96]

For ten years there is no reference to Griffin ap Roberts apart from the pitiful alternation from the register of baptisms to that of burials and the record of his payment of fourpence for the tolling of the bell on the burial day of his son Nicholas ("Receaved for the bell for Goodman Griffins child"). By 1573 things have gone well enough for him to rent a barn in Chapel Street from the council. The rent was seven shillings and threepence per annum, and it is clear that he did not always find it easy to pay. The chamberlains' account, 23 January 1576-7[97] records the receipt from Griffin ap Roberts of two shillings and threepence for rereges. Again in 1589 he pays five shillings and threepence,[98] and a note states that he is to pay two shillings the following quarter. His payment of two shillings is recorded on 16 January 1589-90.[99]

At the hall of 29 March 1592 Griffin ap Roberts is lent five pounds of Oken's money.[100] It would appear that, in spite of the protestations made at Warwick some seventeen years before, the terms of the Oken bond were not being strictly observed, for Griffin ap Roberts was far from being "a new occupier."

Religious differences were threatening to become politically dangerous, for these were the years of John Penry and the Marprelate tracts. Greater still was the danger from Catholic Spain, and the Commissioners for Recusancy had specific instructions to examine recusants on their allegiance to the Queen and their attitude towards the Pope and the King of Spain. In 1592 the Commission reported on church attendance at Stratford-upon-Avon.[101] They found that, amongst others, Griffin ap Roberts did not go monthly to church, but deemed the cause in his case to be "impotency" (i.e. inability through illness). In this same report another Welshman, William Fluellen, and John Shakespeare are said to avoid church for fear of process.[102]

A second list of church-avoiders was made later in the year of 1592 but opposite Griffin ap Roberts's name this time appears the note "now Deade." In the same list it is stated that Robert Griffen, once a recusant, now goes to church, whereas the first list had given him as having been excommunicated near a year since and not seeking to be restored. I have failed to find any indication of his possible connexion with Griffin ap Roberts. He sounds like a son, but in that case he would surely be mentioned in ap Roberts's will. Griffen was a common enough name, and its use in *Piers Plowman* shows that it was regarded in England as a stock name for Welshmen.

The burial register gives 9 August 1592 as the date of Griffin ap Roberts's interment. He must have received good warning of approaching death, for his will was made on 30 July. In it he gave his movable goods and household stuffs equally to his son Thomas ap Roberts and his daughter Margret ap Roberts,[103] to be divided by discretion of his wife Margaret. At the end of the will comes a list of five debts owing to him, the most considerable being one of three pounds owed him by Thomas Price, tinker.[104] The will is signed with a rough cross which may indicate illiteracy or extreme illness.[105] The will was proved on 4 October and an inventory of his goods and chattels was drawn up in April 1593 by five men, one of them a Welshman. Since this document gives us some notion of the possessions of a not very successful shopkeeper of those days, I give it in full.[106]

> The true inventory of the goodes & Cattells of Griphyn Ap Roberts late of Stratford Upon Avon in the countye of Warwycke botcher decessed taken the second day of Apriell in the xxxvth yeare of the Rayngne of our Soverayngne lady Elizabeth by the grace of god Queene of Eyngland, Fraunce and Ierland defender of the Fayth &c by the discretyon of Thomas Godwyne, Wyllyam hobday, Frauncis burnell Thomas Sharp & hu(m)fre Price.
>
> Inp(ri)mis his app(ar)ell P(ri)sed at xxs.
>
> It' in the Chamber vi fether beds, vi flocke beds vi pere of blankets & vi hyllyngs[107] p(ri)sed at vi li.
>
> It' xii boulsters & vi pillows & xiiii pere of sheets   xls
>
> It' iii pere of beddsteds ii coffers & a Cobbord   xiiis iiid in the hall
>
> It' xii candlestycks, xxviii platters, viii sawcers, fyve salts, two counterfet disshes & ii pewter potts   xxs
>
> It' one Chere the seelyng[108] in the howse the portall & two other old Coubbords   vis viiid
>
> It' a pere of Aundyrons a fyer shovell, a pere of tongs & pott hangles   iis
>
> It' in the p(ar)lor fowr Coffers, thre table bords & fowrforms & all the paynted clothes[109]   zs

It' in the kytchyn vii brasse panns, viii Cawdrons and eight brasse potts at   xxxs

It' one bruyng leade[110]   xs

It' thre braches[111] ii pere of Cobbords ii brandards[112]   iiis

It' vi barrells, ii lomes,[113] ii payles ii garners[114] one utyng fate[115] and kyver[116] at   xs

It' in the Shop vi Cleevers & iii knyffes   iiis iiiid

It' one horse p(ri)sed at   xxs

It' a dosen of spones w(i)t(h) disshes & trenchers & other smale Implements   xxd

Som totalis   xvi li[117]

The list is not impressive, yet the furniture was the sort we pay quite a lot for today, and the painted hangings gave colour and life to a functional interior. The beds sound comfortable, but comfort during the day had not yet been thought of, and it is to be noted that he only possessed one chair.

Griffin ap Roberts's wife must have been a careful and honest woman, for it is recorded that on 21 February 1595 ''Margaret Gryffyn wido did likewise bring in'' the five pounds of Oken's money borrowed by her husband in 1592.[118] His widow, wrongly named Jone Griffyn[119] in the inventory of her goods, died some time during 1598 and her inventory was made on 9 March 1599. Her it is. Most of Griffin's furniture and all the butcher's shop equipment have gone to the son and daughter, but the painted cloths have remained in the widow's possession and since they are now said to be old they are probably hangings she brought with her when she was married.

The true Inventorye of the goodes of Jone Griffyn late of Stratford upon Avon in the Countye of Warwycke Wydowe decessed taken the ixth day of March in the forteth & one yeare of the Rayngne of our Soverayne Ladye Elizabeth by the grace of God Queene of Eyngland Fraunce & Ierland defender of the Fayth &c by the discretyon of John Rogers & Wyllyam Emmets, as Followethe

Inp(rimis) her apperrell p(ri)sed at   xiis iiiid

It(em) two pere of blankets ii towells & one old hyllyng praysed at   vis viiid

Ite one Wall bedde ii boulsters and one pyllowe at   xiiis iiiid

It iii pere of sheetes, iiii table clothes two towells two pyllowe bures[120] three table napkyns at   xxvis viiid

Ite one Joyned bedsted thre other bedsteds and fowr coffers at   xxs

It one Joyned table bord one other lyttle table twoe benches, ii formes, ii chyres,[121] a Cubbord w(i)t(h) other smale Implements at   xxxs

It one brasse pott iiii kettles & a skymer at   xiiis iiiid

Ite all the pewter at   xs
It one dosen of Spones a dosen of trenchers wyth Juggs &
Cuppes at   xiid
It a pere of Aundyrons, a brach, a pere of Cobbords, a frying pan,
pott hookes & lynks & a grydyron at   vs
It thre old paynted clothes at   xxd
Som' vii li xiid [122]
(Shown at Stratford-upon-Avon 3 July 1559) [123]

David Jones

I wish there were more to be found about David Jones of Stratford-upon-Avon, for although professional companies of actors visited the town often enough, his is the only name linked with amateur production, and this at a time when William Shakespeare may still have been at Stratford.

David Jones was extremely unlucky in marriage, for during the short period of twelve years he married and buried three wives, together with two of the three sons born to him. Let me first of all assemble chronologically such facts as are provided by the registers of marriages, baptisms, and burials:

1577 June 7	Davy Jones and Elizabeth Queny married. [124]
1578 January 25	Elizabeth wife to David Jones buried with her infant son John.
1579 June 22	David Jones and Frances Hathaway married. [125]
1582 October 14	Humphrey son of David Jones bapt.
1586 August 12	Frances wife to David Jones buried.
1588 September 20	An infant son to David Jones buried. [126]
1589 December 18	Katheren wife to David Jones buried.

A sad record indeed. Let us turn to his public life in Stratford, where the facts offered us are few but of very great interest.

From the first that we see of him, David Jones seems set for such success as Stratford could offer. His first marriage, to Adrian Quyny's daughter, seems to show that this promise was recognized, for the Quynys were one of Stratford's oldest families and Adrian Quyny had by 1574 established his claim to the title of gentleman. [127]

In 1579 David Jones could afford to keep a servant, for the chamberlains' account for 20 January 1579-80 [128] records the sum of fourpence paid to David Jones's man for entering his name in the captain's book. [129]

At the election day hall of 4 September 1583[130] "yt ys agreed that the Chamberlains shall pay Davy[131] Jones thirteen shillings and fourpence towards his expenses at Whytsontyde last." What the expenses incurred were is explained in the subsequent chamberlains' account,[132] where this sum is recorded as having been paid to "Davi Jones and his companye for his pastyme at Whitsontyde." So it was David Jones who produced the Whitsun pastorals to which Perdita refers to charmingly in *The Winter's Tale*, a play in which we have already found a reminiscence of Stratford. And this Whitsuntide pastime was performed when Shakespeare was 19 and, for all we know, still at Stratford. I find it hard to believe that he took no part in it, that he did not even write it for David Jones to produce. And is it too fanciful to find in David Jones the original of Peter Quince, the tactful if inartistic producer of *Pyramus and Thisbe*? Where else but at Stratford did Shakespeare see rude English mechanicals disport themselves in this way? And if it was at Stratford, then David Jones was their producer.

On 2 October 1584 David Jones, whose name is this time given as Davidus James, was elected leather sealer for the coming year.[133] Two leather sealers were appointed every year at Stratford. It was an important office, for the standard of leather production had to be kept up, and it would be David Jones's duty to inspect the shop and materials of John Shakespeare, glover. Two years later, 6 September 1586, he was given the equally important office of aletaster.[134] The quality of the ale sold at Stratford was a constant concern of the council, and innkeepers and tipplers, as sellers of ale were sometimes called, needed regular inspection.

On 17 February 1586-7 David Jones is granted the loan of five pounds of Oken's money, and on the same day acts as surety for Jacob Taylor, who borrows fifty shillings from another fund.[135] He is a dependable young man and on the road to high office under the council. On 6 September 1587 he is elected constable,[136] and for what was to be the most important year of all for constables, that of the Armada threat. This was something much more serious than the occasional musters at Warwick which the Queen commanded, and the gravity of the situation is reflected in the constables' bill for the summer of 1588, which David Jones must have helped to prepare.[137] A long and detailed list is given of supplies and preparations and the cost of it all. There were leather coats for the Stratford soldiers, either eight or twelve in number, flask leathers, daggers and girdles, gunpowder, match for match-lock muskets; charges are included for repairs to much of this equipment; the cost of the carriage for the equipment and the conduct money for the soldiers is set down. The bill is endorsed: ''The constables byll for charges uppon our soldiers 1588.'' William Evans, the armourer, whom we shall meet later, must have had a busy time.

In December 1590 Nicholas Underhill is attached to answer David Jones and the latter makes a deposition against him which is now lost. That is the last we hear of this enterprising young man at Stratford-upon-Avon. Since his burial is not recorded there and there is no further reference to him in the records, it must be taken that he moved to some other place, away from a town which had not been lucky for him, but where he may have played some part in the encouragement of the world's greatest dramatic genius.

Thomas Jenkins

Not much is known about Thomas Jenkins, who was headmaster of the Stratford grammar school from 1573 to 1579, during the impressionable age for the young Shakespeare of from 9 to 15, and to whom Shakespeare owed what Latin and Greek he knew. It is little wonder then that when the dramatist created a schoolmaster in *The Merry Wives of Windsor* he should make him a Welshman.

Jenkins was a member of St. John's College, Oxford. He took his B.A. in 1567 and his M.A. in 1570. He was therefore still a young man when he came to Stratford. Sir Thomas White, founder of John's, had in 1566[138] requested two years leave of absence for Jenkins so that he might teach children. White says that Thomas Jenkins is the son of an old servant of his in London. Jenkins was therefore a London Welshman, and one wonders how much of a Welsh accent he really had, and whether Shakespeare, in creating Sir Hugh Evans, had tacked on to Jenkins an accent of a kind he must have been familiar with at Stratford. One can conceive of a scholarly Welshman pronouncing *big* as *pig*, but would an Oxford M.A. continue to refer to Alexander as the Big? Yet there is a joyous reality about Sir Hugh's Latin lesson that may well spring from a memory. The truth must be that there is no one original for Sir Hugh Evans, any more than there is for Hamlet or Falstaff.

Thomas Jenkins seems to have come to Stratford from Warwick, or at least via Warwick. Our first record of him, showing him to be established in Stratford early in 1574, is his payment of rent to the council for two rooms, at ten shillings and five shillings the year. [139] The chamberlains' account for 14 March 1575-6, [140] just two years after his first appearance in the rent roll, has an item: "pd to the seriauntes [sergeants] for a scholemaster that came from Warwicke." If this refers to Thomas Jenkins, as seems likely, then it records a delayed payment for expenses incurred in reception of the new schoolmaster. Again in this same account Thomas Jenkins is down as having paid the council two shillings and sixpence, being a quarter's rent for one room.

He was probably married at this time, for the register of baptisms records on 19 January 1577 "Thomas sonne to Mr. Thomas Jenkins." Illegitimate children were plainly entered as bastards.

The chamberlains' account for 29 January 1577-8 records a payment to the schoolmaster of twenty pounds for his wages. [141] The chamberlains' account of 16 January 1578-9 shows the payment of half his wages, ten pounds, and on 20 January 1579-80 fifteen pounds are paid to the schoolmaster. The same account gives the payment of ten shillings to Mr Jenkins for the implements and the carriage, and here we come to the end of his career at Stratford. The explanation for this is that he took charge of the men and equipment leaving Stratford for the musters at Warwick in June 1579. It was the end of term, he was leaving Stratford and he took the opportunity of the train band, for which the council then asked him to be responsible.

On 9 July 1579 Thomas Jenkins made out a quittance, or receipt, to John Cotton, who, through the council, paid him six pounds to depart from Stratford. [142] This was John Cottam, his successor as headmaster of Stratford. It has been suggested that Jenkins was not liked at Stratford and that he was thus induced to give up his post, but Cottam only stayed three years and in 1584, two years after Cottam's departure, the schoolmaster's room was still known as "Mr. Ginkins Chamber." [143]

So Thomas Jenkins came and went, arriving from Warwick and returning there, leaving perhaps little impression on Stratford society except the memories and raw material he left with William Shakespeare.

Thomas a Price

Two craftsmen of Stratford, Thomas a Price and William Evans, have left some record of themselves through their dealings with the Stratford council, so it may be as well to separate them from the scores of other Welsh names which occur only once or twice.

Thomas a Price (also spelt Thomas Price and Pryce) was a tinker who marked any documents he had to sign with the symbol of a cock, probably from the many weathercocks he had made. The Thomas Pryce who was buried on 27 September 1587 may have been his father.

John Shakespeare acted as surety to Price for the considerable sum of ten pounds and seems to have lost his money.[144] This was in 1586. At a council meeting of 23 June 1587 Price was granted the twenty years lease of a house in Henley Street, two doors from John Shakespeare, and the lease was sealed, 16 January 1589-90.[145] This house was destroyed in the great fire of 1595. Price did several jobs for the council, including work on the clock face of the High Cross clock, at Market Cross House. For this clock he made a brass hand and soldered on to it a Tudor rose.[146]

We remember that Griffin ap Roberts, in the list of moneys owed him at his death in 1592, included the item: ''Thomas Price Tinker owes me iij li (three pounds).''[147] He would therefore seem to have been able to persuade people to lend him large sums of money without showing much inclination to repay.

I have been able to find no further reference to him, but the burial register records the burying of Ales *uxor* Thomas Price, 7 November 1602.

There were other Prices too at Stratford. Humphrey Price, though Stratford born, the son of John ap Rice, appears only once, apart from the record of his baptism, to prepare the inventory of Griffin ap Roberts. His father's three children are recorded:

1561 April 5	Humfredus filius Johannis Ap rice
1562-3 January 21	Alicia filis Johannis Ap rice
1566 November 7	Catarina filia Johannis Ap rice

This John ap Rice was married in 1559,

1559 November 5	John Aprise to Agnes Daniell

and it would seem likely that the John Price who married Agnes Ward on 1 November 1591 was his son.

Here perhaps should be included the record of another baptism:

1590 June 14	Dorothe daughter to Evans Ryce.

William Evans

William Evans was for years armourer and cutler to the Stratford council. The following are the occasions on which his name is mentioned in the chamberlains' accounts in connexion with this kind of work:

20 January 1579-80 [148]

> paid to William Evans for scowring iiij swordes & mending two caleuers (calivers)   xijd
> paid to William Evans for scowring of the George armoure the vjth day of June [149]   iiijd

26 January 1580-1 [150]

> paid to William Evans for making cleane the Armor & repayring it with buccles and rivettes   xs iiijd
> paid to William Evans the vijth day of October for scowring and mending the trayne mens peeces

31 January 1581-2 [151]

> paid to William Evans for scowringe all the harnes and gunnes   iijs
> paid to William Evans for mending a Coslett (corslet) and scowring two pykes   xiiijd

January 1585-6 [152]

> payd to Wyllyam Yeavans cutler the vijth day of August 1585 for scowrynge the harnes that ys ij corslets viij callyvars for makynge iij pans for one flaske box and mending swords and Daggars   vjs viijd

Jenkins the Beadle—Jenkins the Mason

That of beadle was the least exalted of offices under the corporation. To this post a certain Jenkins was appointed in 1576, and the chamberlains' account for 23 January 1576-7 [153] records the following payments to cover the cost of his outfit:

> paid Goodwife Cope for Jenkins   ijs
> paid for three yards and a half of frysse [154] for Jenkyns coat and a yard and a half of cotton to line it   vs jd
> paid Patrick for making Jankins coat   vjd

We cannot tell whether he is also Jenkins the mason whose boy is

paid one penny according to the chamberlains' account of 1580-1.[155]
Either the mason or the beadle, if they were two persons, is probably
the William Jenkins whose son's baptism is recorded:

 1563 September 9   Gulielmus filius W. Jinekins

We meet this Gulielmus once more, in the register of marriages:

 1600 May 18   William Jenkins to Mary Emmete

Lewis Davies

The Stratford Court of Record MSS[156] record an action taken
against Lewis Davys by John Rogers. Jurors were appointed to
inquire whether Lodovicke Davys did deliver to Edward Ingram[157]
two double dozen of black conies for John Rogers. One wonders what
the forty-eight black rabbits were for and where Lewis Davies got
them, if he was not a rabbit breeder. Document no. 132 gives a
demurrer in this action, no. 133 the defence of Lewis Davies, and no.
134 the bill of costs. All this happened in 1599.

In 1602 Ralph Ellis is required to answer Lodovicus Davies concerning a loan of twenty shillings.[158] This Ralph Ellis may be the son
of Robert Ellis, whose daughter Maria was baptized in 1571. Lewis
Davies may have been the son of a Thomas Davies.[250]

Robert Lewis

It is impossible to distinguish Robert Lewis, if there was such a
person, from Lewis ap Williams, who, as we have seen, was sometimes called by this name. To make matters worse, Robert Lewis is
once referred to as Robert Williams, so that here again we may have
the respected alderman.[160] The case in which this happened occurred
in the winter of 1594-5 and it does not at first thought seem likely that
Lewis ap Williams would fall into such stubborn debt when he was
old and honoured unless a matter of principle was involved. Again we
do not easily recognize Lewis ap Wiliams in the Robert Lewis who
fathered an illegitimate child on a girl called Getly in 1586,[161] when
he was getting on for sixty. But even here a man of principle is concerned, for it was very rare for a father to acknowledge an illegitimate
child in this way at its baptism, as was done in this case,

We must accord to Robert Lewis an unproved identity, but even
if all that is known of him be added to what we know of Lewis ap

Williams, I do not think our respect for the alderman is sensibly diminished.

Still other Lewises occur in the records. The register of baptisms gives us:

1558 December 25   Richard Lewis son to Williams Lewis

The marriage register gives:

1565 January 29   Hugo Lewice et Jana Lette

And there is a mention of a John Lewis.[161]

The Ap Johns

The Ap Johns, also known as up John, Upjohn, ap Jones, and ap Johnson, do not seem to have distinguished themselves at Stratford otherwise than through birth, procreation, and death. I will list the known facts.

Register of baptisms:

1566 April 3   Nicholaus filius Hugonis ap Johnson[163]
1567 February 21   Thomas filius Hugonis Apjohn
1572 February 21   Johannes filius Hugonis ap Jones
1598 August 16   Anthonius filius Richardi Hues up John
1599-1600 January 28 Johannes filius Richardi Up John als Hues[164]

Register of marriages:

1588 November 30   Nicholas up John & Elizabeth Payne
1594 October 18   Richard up John & Margret: Jams
                      Woodwards mayd

Register of burial:

1590 October 11   Ursula daughter of Hugh up John

I think it likely that this Hugh ap John is the carpenter to whom as Hugh Jones the council makes a payment of sixteen pence for work done on the floor of the council chamber in 1580.[165]

The Hughes

Apart from the Ap John tangle there are other occurrences of the name Hughes at Stratford. A Richard Hughes, Richardus Hews in the register, was buried on 23 April 1573, and in the next chamberlains' account comes the item:

Recd for ringing of the bell for Hews   iiijd

He is not to be confused with Richard Hughes ap John.

In 1574 Thomas Hewes rents a house in Church Street from the council for twenty shillings the year. And the burial register records the interment of Anne *uxor* Thome Hewes.

On 28 April 1589 Jone, daughter to William Hewes was baptized.

The Joneses

Jones was the commonest of all Welsh names, the commonest of all names, for that matter, at Stratford in Shakespeare's day, but of them all only David Jones emerged into any kind of limelight. Hugonis ap Jones and Hugh Jones I have already taken to be Hugh ap John, but there were besides Richard Jones, Thomas Jones, John Jones, Edward Jones, Robert Jones, and William Jones. Here are the Joneses as they come up in the records.

Register of baptisms:

1568 October 6	Anna filia Johannis Jones
1575 August 16	Richard sonne to Thomas Jones
1576 November 19	Stephen sonne to Thomas Jones
1579 August 5	Katherine daughter to Thomas Jones
1582 February 25	Grace daughter to Thomas Jones
1584 May 12	Margret daughter to Thomas Jones
1586 May 11	Ffrancis daughter to Richard Jones[166]
1587 September 22	Edmund son to Thomas Jones
1590 March 12	David son to Edward Jones
1592 May 21	Jone daughter to Thomas Jones
1599 November 5	Griffen filius Roberti Jones

Register of marriages:

1565 August 4	Johannes Jones et Cicilia Cottrell vidua
1572 January 18	John Jones to Ursula Salsbury
1574 October 5	Thomas Jones & Ales Ensdale
1574 November 21	Robert Jones & Sicelye Holands
1580 August 8	John Morris & Elnor Jones[167]
1583 November 10	Richard Jones & Anne Barret
1585 January 18	John Jones & Elizabeth Ffakener
1585 November 15	William Jones & Margret Eaton
1586 August 2	Thomas Jones & Annys Clarke
1589 June 25	Edward Jones & Elizabeth Johnsons
1598 December 21	Robert Jones to Elizabeth Ffish

Of all these Joneses, only John Jones and his second wife Ursula are recorded as buried at Stratford:

1575 December 5   Ursula wife to John Jones
1601 August 17   Johannis Joanes a Wellesman (Welshman)

Edwards and Ap Edward

According to the rent roll of 10 March 1573-4[168] John Edwards, sometimes called John Welsh, paid five shillings for a tenement which he held from the council and held a house in Church Street which he rented to Richard Hill for eight shillings a year. The register of baptisms gives him a daughter called Anna (filia Johannis Edwards) baptized 25 May 1562. Three days before that the register records:

1562 May 19   Johannes filius Mazicij Ap Edwards

I take this mysterious name to be a version of Morris ap Edward, who was married in 1558:

1558 May 14   Morris Apedward & Agnes Millis

Morris Evans

The name of Morris Evans occurs five times in the registers and nowhere else.

Register of marriages:
1588 January 14   Morris Evans & Bredgit Smith
1601 November 1   Morris Evans to Ann Mayo

Register of baptisms:

1590 August 30   Elnor daughter to Morris Evans
1592 November 13   Catherina filia Morres Evans
1598 April 16   Wilhelmus filius Moris Evans

Other Names

Here, finally, are names which occur only once or twice.

Register of baptisms:

1571 January 5   Maria filia Roberti Ellys
1583 November 4   John sonne to Hugh Apowell
1584 November 30   Ursula daughter to Howell Apowell[169]
1586 December 29   Elizabeth daughter to John Owen
1590 July 12   William sonne to Robert Williams[170]
1593 September 21   Catherina filia Edwardi Powell

Register of marriages:

1574 June 6	George Welshman & Anne Awood[171]
1575 October 23	Thomas Davyes & Ales Cooke
1582 May 6	Hugh Uppowell & Sibell Hyll
1584 June 30	John ap Roberts to Annys Nicholes[172]
1591 October 11	Griffen ap Thomas et Elnor Bewante
1597 September 21	Thomas Cowrt to Alice Morice

Then there was a Thomas Welshman who is given as a council tenant in the survey of corporation property of 1582,[173] and, of course, William Fluellen. The name of William Fluellen[174] we now from the recusancy report of 1592, where he is bracketed with John Shakespeare as a church-avoider on 9 July 1595. Shakespeare used this name for his excellent Welsh captain in Henry V, but the character of Captain Fluellen he must have observed elsewhere than at Stratford, probably in London and chiefly in the person of Sir Roger Williams. This outstanding professional soldier was the Earl of Essex's tutor and guide in the art of war, and Shakespeare must have met him or heard a good deal about him at Essex House or at the Earl of Southampton's. Sir Roger was not only a great soldier but a theorist of war, and the title of one of his published works shows much similarity to Fluellen's discursive style: *A Brief Discourse of War with his opinion concerning some part of Martial Discipline* (London, 1590, quarto).

Other odd occurrences of the names Evans, Edwards, Roberts, Davies, Nicholas, and Hopkins, not being indubitably Welsh, i.e. not having the *ap* or an unmistakable Welsh Christian name, I have not recorded, especially when they are not linked with any person or event of interest or importance in the life of Stratford-upon-Avon. Yet these other names do accentuate the feeling of a considerable Welsh element in Stratford's population which one cannot fail to get in going through these records.

It has already been said that few of these Stratford Welshmen attained eminence in the public life of the town. It is equally true that few, if any, of them were sufficiently improvident to become a drain on the town's charity. The Stratford almshouses provided accommodation for twenty-four old people, but it is rare to find a Welsh name amongst the inmates. In the alms list of 23 December 1596 there is no Welsh name,[175] but a John Davys, who may or may not have been a Welshman, was admitted at the council meeting of 3 June 1597.[176]

Some Welsh families, notably those of Lewis ap Williams and Griffin ap Roberts, were permanently resident at Stratford. Many other Welshmen found wives there but did not stay long enough to be buried. Only a search of the records of such places as Wellesbourne, Hampton Lucy, Alcester, and Warwick will show how far these other Welshmen stayed on in the Midlands. I suspect that many of them did stay, to become completely anglicized, except for certain recognizable names, during the seventeenth century. And by this time they are interesting to us only in their numbers, not as individuals. The only one of these lost Stratford Welshmen whose subsequent life would promise to be of interest is David Jones, producer of amateur theatricals.

Acknowledgements

I wish to thank the Shakespeare Birthplace Trustees for access to the library and to the manuscripts in their possession, and for permission to make use of hitherto unprinted material; and the Director and his Assistant for the ready and learned help they gave me.

[1] 2 Henry IV c. 12.

[2] Ibid c. 20.

[3] Though Henry VI's confirmation of all statutes against Welshmen was not formally repealed until 1624 (21 Jac. I c. 28 par. 11).

[4] and [5] Salzman and Styles, *History of Warwickshire*, O.U.P., 1945, Vol. III, p. 336, n. 21.

[6] Sheep Street.

[7] View of frankpledge, 5 October 1560, Dug. Soc., I. pp. 102 f. (Many of the important documents between 1553 and 1592 have been printed in the four volumes of the *Minutes and Records of the Corporation of Stratford-upon-Avon*, published by the Dugdale Socciety. When the document referred to appears in these volumes, I shall indicate it as above. Otherwise I shall refer to the original document.) View of frankpledge was a relic of Saxon times, a periodical consideration of the rights and duties of the members of a community and of breaches of regulations.

[8] The following versions of his name appear in the records: Lewes upp Willm. Lewes up Willyams, Lewes ap William, Lodwico ap Wyllyam, Lews ap William, Lowdoic ap Willm, Lodwic ap Willm, Lodowicc ap Willm, Lodowycus ap Wyllyam, Lodwicus ap Wyllyam, Leywys, Mr Lews, Mr Lewes, Lewes ap Wyllyams, Ludouicus upwilliams, Lewis ap Williames, Mr Lewis Williams, Loddoig Lewes, and Lodovicus ap Williams. In addition, references to a Robert Lewes may be intended for him.

[9] View of frankpledge as above.

[19] Possibly the Robert Lewes mentioned as a householder in the 1553 Charter of Incorporation. Dug. Soc., I, p. 7.

[11] Dug. Soc., I, p. 23.

[12] Concern with this danger to the town's finances appears frequently in the minutes. A fatherless child could be a serious burden on the charity of the town.

[13] Reports of these early meetings in the life of the borough are headed: "Visus ffranci plegii cum Curia et Sessione Pacis . . ." The functions of court leet, view of frankpledge, and council are confused in a way which is typical of the growth of English institutions during these early years. Later meetings, from 1563 on, are called "halls" and all these functions merge into that of the borough council.

[14] Dug. Soc., I, pp. 44-8.

[15] Dug. Soc., I, pp. 62-6

[16] Cf. John Shakespeare's experience with Griffin ap Roberts during the winter of 1558-9, for which see later. Shakespeare's *Much Ado about Nothing* gives a comic but accurate picture of the activities of the Stratford constables and the company they called together.

[17] "Item presentimus quod Ricardus Cutt qui de domino tenuit libere per cartam unum tenementum cum pertinentiis in Stretford in quodam vico ibidem vocato the High Stret per Redditum inde domino per Annum jd citra ultimam curiam alienavit predictum tenementum cum pertinentiis cuidam lodwico ap Wullyam et heredibus suis qui quidam lodwicus presens in Curia fecit domino fidelitatem pro premissis." Dug. Soc., I, p. 61.

[18] I.e. qualified townsman elected to the Council.

[19] Dug. Soc., I, pp. 69-75.

[20] Ibid., I, pp. 80-5

[21] Now Scholars Lane.

[22] Ibid., I, p. 90. John Shakespeare was elected constable at this meeting.

[23] Ibid., I, pp. 91-6.

[24] Copied from the MS. *Misc. Doc.*, VII, p.39.

[25] Ibid, VII, p. 56.

[26] Council book A, p. 5. This page is reproduced in Dug. Soc., I, p. 134.

[27] Council book A, p. 301.

[28] Dug. Soc., I, p. 105.

[29] Ibid., I, pp. 115-9.

[30] Ibid., I, p. 130. There is no explanation given for this debt, for the Chamberlains who presented their account sixteen days before this were John Shakespeare and John Taylor. This debt to Lewis ap Williams is recorded as paid in the Chamberlains' account of 21 March 1564-5.

[31] Ibid., I, p. 130. He is here referred to as Mr. Lewes. Also ibid., I. p. 133. He is here referred to as Mr. Lewes. Also ibid., I. p. 133.

[32] Ibid., I, p.134.

[33] Ibid., I, pp. 137-41.

[34] Richard Sharpe was Sergeant at Mace to the Council.

[35] Dug. Soc., I, p. 141.

[36] Ibid., I, pp. 144-5.

[37] Ibid., I, pp. 145-6.

[38] Ibid., II, p. 6.

[39] Ibid., II, p. 8.

[40] "Johannes filius Lodovici Apwilliams domi bapt et illico mortua."

[41] Dug. Soc., II, p. 31.

[42] Ibid., II, p. 52.

[43] A well-to-do miller of Bidford near Temple Grafton, who had many connections with Stratford. See E. I. Fripp, *Shakespeare's Haunts,* p. 49 and note.

[44] The little common belonging to the town which ran alongside the river between the bridge and the present-day theatre.

[45] Dug. Soc., II, p. 72.

[46] Ibid., II, p. 78.

[47] I.e. tithe.

[48] Many such visits of professional players are recorded during these years.

[49] Fire ladders.

[50] Dug. Soc., II, pp. 95-9.

[51] Ibid., II, p. 88. We remember that a Robert Lewes occurs in the charter as a householder.

[52] Ibid., II, p. 93.

[53] Ibid., II, p. 92.

[54] Ibid., II, pp. 103-7.

[55] A fire hook was used to pull down burning roofs and walls to check the spread of a fire.

[56] Dug. Soc., II, p. 107.

[57] Ibid., III, p. 13.

[58] A pleasant aroma of hot spiced drinks often arises from these records.

[59] Dug. Soc., III, p. 24.

[60] Ibid., III, p. 57.

[61] Ibid., III, p. 97.

[62] Sir John Hubande of Ipsley was steward to the Earls of Warwick and Leicester and visited Stratford on behalf of the lord of the manor. The College of the Holy Trinity had been dissolved under the Chantries Act and the building had become the property of the council.

[63] Roughly a dozen to fifteen bottles.

[64] *W.T.*, IV, iii, ll. 60-6.

[65] Dug. Soc., III, p. 123.

[66] Ibid., III, p. 129.

[67] Ibid., III, p. 140.

[68] Ten pounds ten shillings.

[69] Dug Soc., III, p. 141.

[70] An entry of 22 September 1561 gives: "Agnes filius Hugonis ap Williams bapt." It would therefore seem possible that Lewis ap Williams had two brothers, Robert and Hugh, in Stratford in the early sixties. The only two references to the Robert Williams above which I have been able to find are the entry of his marriage to Mary Sawbridge on 12 January 1581 and an action taken by William Perry in 1594 against Robert Williams *alias* Lewis (just to confuse it further). See *Misc. Doc.*, VI, No. 188 (Court of Record).

[71] Dug. Soc., IV, p. 15.

[72] He was the lessee but he obtained the council's permission to relet the house. Ibid., IV, p. 30.

[73] Ibid., IV, p. 45.

[74] An entry in the marriage register for 17 January 1579 records the marriage of William Wilson and Anne Hathaway of Shotterye, obviously not Shakespeare's wife to be, who might have been an Agnes Hathaway of Shottery.

[75] Dug. Soc., IV, p. 53.

[76] Council book A 350.

[77] Council book B 9.

[78] Council book B 20. There are only two marks left now and they are rough crosses of the perhaps illiterate. Richard Quyny signs beautifully and Alexander Aspinall, the schoolmaster, in a strong angular, backward sloping hand.

[79] Council book B 41.

[80] Council book B 43.

[81] Council book B 46.

[82] Council book B 50.

[83] Aubrey MSS., No. 4, p. 78 (Bodleian Library). Facsimile in Halliwell's *Works of Shakespeare* (1853), Vol. I, p. 76.

[84] and [85] Thomas and Margret were alive when Griffin died and are mentioned in his will (see below). Of William there is no further trace.

[86] Dug. Soc., I, p. 30.

[87] Ibid., I, p. 94.

[88] John Shakespeare was one of these.

[89] Francis Harbadge was a skinner and victualler of Corn Street.

[90] Dug. Soc., I, p. 90.

[91] Ibid., I, pp. 115-9.

[92] Court of Record MSS., Vol. I, No. 190.

[93] No. 234.

[94] No. 218.

[95] No. 232.

[96] No. 235. This Henry Rogers was afterwards for years steward and clerk to the council.

[97] Dug. Soc., II, p. 114.

[98] Ibid., IV, p. 69.

[99] Ibid., IV, p. 78.

[100] Ibid., IV, p. 148.

[101] Ibid., IV, p. 149.

[102] I.e. arrest for debt. Too much has been made of recusancy on the part of Shakespeare's father, for no one has been able to decide whether he leant towards Puritanism or Popery. Fear of arrest for debt gives a valid reason for his apparent nonconformity.

[103] Note the retention of the *ap* at a time when it was generally being given up, and even, against strict accuracy, in his daughter's surname.

[104] See Thomas Price below.

[105] Will of Griffin ap Roberts. Misc. Doc., Vol. VI, No. 67.

[106] Misc. Doc., Vol. I, No. 12.

[107] Bed covers.

[108] Ceiling?

[109] Cloths or wall hangings.

[110] Brewing vat.

[111] Broach or roasting spit.

[112] Grills or frying pans.

[113] Looms?

[114] Salt storing place.

[115] Wetting vat for the first process of brewing.

[116] Cover.

[117] Sixteen pounds.

[118] Council book B 9.

[119] She may of course have been the wife of Robert Griffen, or Margaret Griffin may have been carelessly misnamed by association with Jone, wife of the other well-known Welshman, Lewis ap Williams. This is no stranger than the confusion between Anne Whateley and Anne Hathaway in the records of Shakespeare's marriage.

[120] Covers.

[121] Chairs; one more than Griffin possessed.

[122] Seven pounds twelvepence.

[123] Misc. Doc., Vol. I, No. 41.

[124] Adrian Quyny's daughter. The various spellings of this name suggest that it was pronounced Queeny.

[125] Hathaway was not an uncommon name in Stratford and its environs and she was not necessarily closely related to Shakespeare's wife. Yet they may have been cousins or even sisters.

[126] This suggests that his third marriage, to Catherine, took place late in 1587, though not at Stratford.

[127] Dug. Soc., II, p. 87.

[128] Ibid., III, pp. 40-50.

[129] Recruitment for the October musters at Warwick.

[130] Ibid. III, p. 129.

[131] His name is spelt Davy, closer to Dafydd than David is, as often as not.

[132] Ibid., III, p. 137.

[133] Dug. Soc., III, p. 141.

[134] Ibid., III, p. 170.

[135] Ibid., IV, p. 20.

[136] Ibid., IV, p. 24.

[137] Ibid., IV, p. 39.

[138] Letter quoted, Dug. Soc., II, p. xl.

[139] Ibid., II, p. 86.

[140] Ibid., II, p. 103-7.

[141] Twenty pounds a year was a very good salary for those days, better than that paid at many other grammar schools. Under the Gild the salary had been ten pounds, but it was doubled when the council took the school over; ibid., III, p. 13.

[142] Dug. Soc., III, p. 33.

[143] Ibid., III, p. 150.

[144] See E. I. Fripp, *Richard Quyny*, p. 102, n. 2.

[145] Dug. Soc., IV, p. 82.

[146] Chamb. Acct., Dug. Soc., III, pp. 40-50.

[147] See p. 47.

[148] Dug. Soc., III, p. 45.

[149] This is too soon after the parade of the St. George's Day pageant armour for the cleaning to be in preparation for that annual event. The suggestion has been made that this old armour was pressed into service for the musters and was carried to Warwick on the day of Thomas Jenkins's departure. In that case it was of as much use as our present-day civil defence.

[150] Dug. Soc., III.

[151] Ibid., III, p. 97.

[152] Ibid., III, p. 162.

[153] Ibid., II.

[154] Frieze, a woollen material much associated with Welsh dress.

[155] Dug. Soc., III, pp. 76-85.

[156] Vol. II, No. 130.

[157] Of "fysh not holsum" memory.

[158] Misc. Doc., VI, No. 125.

[159] The register of marriages gives: "1575 October 23 Thomas Davyes and Ales Cooke."

[160] Misc. Doc., VI, No. 188. Robert Williams *alias* Lewis is attached to answer William Perrye for a debt of four shillings for sundry pieces of beef, mutton, and pork. This was not a question of non-payment for meat supplied but rather a dispute over prices and the case brought about a regulation fixing prices.

[161] Register of baptisms: "Julian Getly daughter to Robert Lewis a bastard."

[162] Dug. Soc., I, p. 130.

[163] ap Johnson, Apjohn, and Ap Jones are clearly the same person.

[164] This Richard may have been the son of the above Hugh ap John, here caught hesitating between English and Welsh nomenclature at a time when the latter was being given up.

[165] Dug. Soc., III, pp. 76-85.

[166] Obviously not the above son to Thomas Jones.

[167] A rare case of both parties having Welsh names. Welshmen usually married English wives and there are not many Welsh girls in the records.

[168] Dug. Soc., II, p. 80.

[169] I take Hugh and Howell Ap Howell to be the same person.

[170] See above for confusion with Robert Lewis and Lewis ap Williams.

[171] Men called Welsh or Welshman were in fact Welsh, though George is not a likely Welsh name in the sixteenth century.

[172] Two sons of Griffin ap R. named John died young. Is this a third?

[173] Dug. Soc., III, p. 106.

[174] Anglicized from Llywelyn.

[175] Council book B 35.

[176] Council book B 40.

Troelus a Chresyd: A Welsh Tragedy

A feature programme which I prepared for the BBC and which was broadcast by the Welsh Regional Service on 19 March 1954, and the subsequent performance of *Troelus a Chresyd*[1] at the National Eisteddfod at Ystradgynlais on 6 August 1954, drew the attention of the Welsh people to their possession of a full-length tragedy of considerable interest and importance. Its existence had been known for some time to a handful of scholars, but its acting possibilities and literary value had been completely ignored. Let us consider what treatment had previously been accorded to this play and what references made to it.

The attention of J.O. Halliwell, the great Shakespearian scholar and archaeologist, was drawn to the play in 1862, and the following manuscript letter is now loosely kept within the covers of Peniarth MS 106 at the National Library of Wales:

> No. 6 St. Mary's Place
> West Brompton
> 25 Feb[y] 1862

Sir,

   It is most particularly kind of you giving me an opportunity (which I need not say I shall gladly seize) of seeing the MS, but I cannot think of naming my own day, and as I am often in Town, I will take my chance of finding it convenient, and it is of no consequence if I have to call many times before I am so fortunate.

> With sincere respect,
> I am Sir,
> yr obed[t] serv[t]
> J. O. Halliwell

It is not stated to whom this letter was addressed, but it must have

been to the owner of the manuscript at that time, W.W.E. Wynne,
Member of Parliament, antiquarian and chairman of the Cambrian
Archaeological Association. Wynne inherited the Hengwrt MSS in
1859, and from 1860 until his death he worked on them and
catalogued them.[2] In 1859 Wynne removed the Hengwrt MSS to
Peniarth, but it is clear from Halliwell's letter that what we now know
as Peniarth MS 106 was in London in February 1862, brought there
perhaps for examination by English scholars. But even if Halliwell
examined the manuscript, and I know of no evidence that he did, he
could have made little of it, for he knew no Welsh and no translation
of *Troelus a Chresyd* existed.

J.G. Evans, for the purposes of the *Report on Manuscripts in the
Welsh Language*, does not pretend to have examined *Troelus a Chresyd*
very closely, nor was it his immediate duty to do so, and he describes
it thus: "Troilus and Cressida, a Welsh Interlude. . . . This Interlude
is divided into V books like *Troilus and Criseyde* in Chaucer, from
whom the opening lines are certainly translated. But all the rest
seems, from a brief inspection, to be such a free paraphrase that it is
not easy to detect anything approaching a translation".[3]

The first serious attempt at the evaluation of *Troelus a Chresyd*
was made by the great American medieval scholar, J.S.P. Tatlock. In
1911 he examined the manuscript, left a note in it to say that he had
done so[4] and published his findings in England and America. Under
the title "A Welsh Troilus and Cressida" in the *Modern Language
Review* (1915), pp. 265-82, he gave an account of the manuscript and
its contents. In a longer paper in the *Publications of the Modern Language
Association of America*, XXX, pp. 673-770, he analysed the accounts
we have of the siege of Troy in Elizabethan literature and placed the
Welsh play in relation to other contemporary versions of the story. He
was able to do this with the help of H. Brython Hughes and E. Stanton
Roberts, who made him a summary, with translations, of the Welsh
text. The play as a whole was summarized, and those sections for
which no source has been found in other versions were translated in
full. The result was a careful and valuable comparative study of the
elements of this great tale as they are to be found in the different
versions. But Tatlock went further than this in essaying some critical
judgments on the Welsh play as drama and literature, which, owing
to his ingorance of Welsh, are quite without value. He refers to the
author as a mountaineer with some knowledge of the classics and
states that the play must have been written for a primitive audience
by one with "little sense for a dramatic situation". He thought the

author had seen an English play on this subject in London and was now "with somewhat artless enthusiasm rushing into imitation". He indicates points at which the author might have treated his material more dramatically, and one of these suggestions will be considered later. Shakespeare, of course, has a long history of "improvement" by critics. Tatlock's opinion of the importance of the play would seem to be summed up in his remark that "the author may one day be identified if anyone thinks him worth identifying" (*Modern Language Review*, X, p. 282), and in a note to this offers Thomas Jones, John Owen, and Edmund Price as possible authors. In spite of this, Tatlock's final note says: "The work is interesting enough, perhaps, in the history of Welsh and English literature, to deserve to be fully published in the original, with a translation" (*Modern Language Review*, X, p. 282, note).

With even less justification and much less knowledge than Tatlock, Anatole le Braz had already made a more sweeping dismissal of *Troelus a Chresyd* from serious consideration as drama. "En Galles, l'*anterlwt* [*sic*] englobe aussi bien les mystères que les moralités ou les farces: il comprend même les ouvrages poétiques dont on ne saisit guère le rapport avec le théâtre. C'est ainsi que l'on trouve rangé dans la catégorie des *anterlwt* un *Troilus et Cressida* qui n'est qu'une traduction libre, et nullement dramatisée, du poème de Chaucer". How surprised M. le Braz would have been had he visited Ystradgynlais in August 1954, when "un rapport avec le théâtre" was convincingly established for this neglected play.

T. Gwynn Jones recognized *Troelus a Chresyd* as a work of some especial interest. In his *Llên Cymru*, III (1926), he printed the prologue and three short excerpts from the body of the play, noting the manuscript source and the title but giving no indication of its dramatic form, the shorter excerpts being printed as independent lyrics. In his foreword to this excellent little anthology he speculated thus: "Pair llawer o'r deunydd i ddyn ofyn cwestiynau — er enghraifft, onid gwell i lenyddiaeth Gymraeg pe cymerasai'r beirdd lwybr y gerdd i 'Droelus a Chresyd', o ran deunydd a mesurau?" (Much of the material makes a man ask questions — for example, would it not have been better for Welsh literature if the poets had taken the path to *Troelus a Chresyd*, in the matter of material and metre?) Daring words for a professor of Welsh in our Welsh University, words which I feel sure are still considered wildly heretical, but showing no awareness of the work as a play or of the exciting paths along which Welsh drama might have moved.

In 1932, Mr W. Beynon Davies successfully offered a thesis on *Troelus a Chresyd* for the degree of M.A. (Wales). In this thesis a careful analysis is made, much more detailed than that of Professor Tatlock, of the Welsh author's indebtedness to other versions of the story. But again I cannot find the general conclusions acceptable. Once more the dramatic possibilities of the play are ignored and the author's varied experiments in free metrical forms are dismissed in these words: "Nid oes grefft yn y byd ar y mydriad.... Rhyw lusgo'n dramgwyddus ymlaen". (There is no craftsmanship at all in the versification.... A stumbling dragging on.) I hope to be able to show, if only by quotation, the inadequacy of this judgment.

The play has been referred to by Miss Elsbeth Evans in these words: "Un o'r testunau anterliwd cynharaf yw *Troelus a Chressyd*, sydd yn dangos bod traddodiad o ddramâu wedi codi yn ymdrin â storïau bydol a chwedlonol: fod rhywun wedi ysgaru'r ddrama oddi wrth grefydd, ac ugeiniau wedi dilyn ei esiampl yn llawen". [6] Here is generalizing from the particular with a vengeance, for this swallow never came near to making a summer and, far from being in any kind of tradition, is a fortunate freak, a unique and unrepeated, unimitated adventure in writing.

Mr Brinley Rees has mentioned "y gerdd faith sydd ar Droelus a Chresyd" [7] (the long poem on Troelus and Cresyd). He thus follows previous opinion and practice, notably that of A. le Braz and T. Gwynn Jones, in taking *Troelus a Chresyd* as a poem rather than as a play. Mr Rees's concern is with the matter rather than with the metre of early Welsh writing in the free measures, and it would therefore be unfair to take him to task for neglecting to consider the interesting experiments in free stanza forms to be found in the play.

Troelus a Chresyd exists in one manuscript only, Peniarth MS 106, now in the National Library of Wales, Aberystwyth. The manuscript, which contains nothing but this play, is in the hand of the industrious John Jones, Gelli Lyfdy. On page 119, roughly half way through the manuscript, the copyist tells us: "Ac fal hyn y terfyna y rann yma or llyfr hunn die mercur y 14 dydd o fis Chwefror yn y vlwyddyn o oedran Kris 1613". (And thus ends this part of this book Wednesday the fourteenth day of February in the year of Christ's age 1613.) For some reason unknown to us, John Jones was in prison a good deal about this time and may not have had the original by him, nine years passed before the manuscript was completed or brought to its present state of completion. [8] His next note is on page 160: "Ac fal hynn y terfyna y 4 llyfr or hanes honn y II dydd o fis Medi yn y vlwyddyn o oedran Krist 1622''. (And thus ends the fourth book of this tale, the eleventh day of September in the year of Christ's age 1622.) Finally, on p. 230, comes the note: ''Diwedd y llyfr. Ac fal hynn y terfyna y 5 llyfr ar diwaethaf or hanes honn y 5 dydd o fis hyddfref oet Krist 1622''. (The end of the book. And thus ends the fifth book of this tale, the fifth day of October, Christ's age, 1622.)

John Jones wrote in a good clear hand, but, in addition to the effect of the later ink, the manuscript does present difficulties. Pp. 79-88 are blank and pp. 85-8 remain uncut to this day. At this point in the work the author depends on Chaucer and the corresponding material omitted at this stage in his following of *Troilus and Criseyde* amounts to 1,300 lines of Chaucer's poem. The play does not suffer by this omission, but the blank pages set a problem for which there are several possible solutions, not one of them entirely satisfactory. Then again, p. 59 has only a great white capital A set in a black ground, whilst p. 60 is blank. But this is the beginning of Act II and no doubt the scribe meant to return and make some special use of this blank space. There are other things which he left undone, meaning to return to them. From p. 39 to p. 119 he omitted all speech headings and all proper names in the text, probably with the intention of doing them later in a different ink, red for speech headings and black underlined with red for other proper names. This does not cause the confusion which might at first be expected, for the speeches are usually fairly easy to allot to their speakers and names of places, gods and humans, within the speeches can usually be tracked down in Chaucer. It is possible therefore that John Jones was copying a play which was not complete and which may not at the time of copying have been performed, but he would hardly have embarked upon its copying unless the work was before 1613 at least as complete as we have it today.

Since stories of Troy were in vogue during the last years of the sixteenth and early years of the seventeenth century, and since our Welsh dramatist was almost certainly following this fashion and had most probably been to see a Trojan play in London late in the 1590s, the most likely time for the writing of *Troelus a Chresyd* is the period 1600-1610. More detailed reference will be made later to books written about Troy and their dates of publication.

I have spoken of *Troelus a Chresyd* as a play, whereas in Welsh it has often been referred to as *cerdd*, a poem, and the copyist himself calls it *hanes*, a tale. And it is divided into five books, not acts, for the author is influenced by Chaucer's division of his peom into five books, though the Welsh play takes the tale far beyond Chaucer's handling of it. But there is no doubt that it was intended for some kind of stage. It is entirely in dialogue, interspersed with comment at the beginning and end of the acts by *Rhagddoedydd*, who acts throughout as prologue and chorus. Throughout the play there are stage directions written in red ink, either alongside the speech or between speeches and ruled off by heavy black lines. Here are some specimens of these directions:

> p. 6   Kalkas yn dywedyd wrtho ei hun. (Kalkas speaking to himself.)
>
> p. 12   Priaf yn galw ir unlle Hector Paris Eneas Antenor Helenws a Throelys i ddoedyt i meddylie pwy un ore ai rhoddi Helen adref ai peidio. (Priaf calls to one place Hector, Paris, Eneas, Antenor, Helenws and Troelus for them to speak their minds whether it is better to let Helen go home or not.)

When the Trojan council calls for Cresyd a stage direction in red on the opposite page says: "Kressyd yn dyfod gida Synon ag yn syrthio ar i glinieu" (p. 25) (Kressyd coming in with Synon and falling on her knees). And during her trial comes the direction: "Troelus yn dywedyd yn issel yng hlyst i vrawd Hector" (p. 32) (Troelus speaking quietly into his brother Hector's ear). Soon after, on p. 34, comes the interesting note to a Troelus speech heading, a helpful note, I imagine, to the actor taking this part: "ag ar hynn mae yn syrthio mewn kariad" (and now he falls in love). At the end of this scene, when Cresyd has been pardoned, Hector's speech heading has the direction: "wrth Kressyd wedi y llaill ymado" (to Kressyd after the others have gone out). Later, on p. 146, comes: "Troylus ai gleddef noeth yn ei law yn ymkanu ei ladd ei hunan" (Troelus with his naked sword in his hand intending to kill himself). But the direction which clinches the argument is that on p. 202: "Diomedes ar yr ystaeds a Chressyd yn dyfod yno" (Diomedes on the stage and Kressyd coming there). The use of the word stage for a platform on which to perform plays was new even in English and this must be the first use of the word in Welsh.

A play in five acts, therefore, intended for performance on a stage, though hardly a professional stage, for no such theatre existed for the production of Welsh plays. Open-air performance is not to be ruled out, and it must be remembered that English mystery plays were performed at Chester until about 1600 and pageants well after that date. To me, however, another atmosphere is suggested by the first line Rhagddoedydd speaks to open the play, a line for which there is no counterpart in Chaucer:

> Chwchwi rasysol gwmpeini, yr achos om dyfodiad yma
> Ydyw y ddangos prudder mab brenin Troya . . .

> (You, gracious company, the reason for my coming here
> is to show the sadness of the son of Troy's king.)

The dramatist has no need to appeal for silence, as Twm o'r Nant was forced to do later. He is confident of a sympathetic hearing from the gracious company he faces. The play was surely meant for performance at a gentleman's house and the prologue's quiet introduction of it is to a cultured group of guests, not to Tatlock's primitive audience. The flourishing of public theatres in London towards the end of the sixteenth century should not cause us to forget that plays and entertainments were far more often performed in the dining halls of schools and colleges, at the Inns of Court, at the Queen's Court, and in great houses in London and throughout the country than on the public stage. The play within the play in Shakespeare's *Hamlet*, Pyramus and Thisbe in *A Midsummer Night's Dream*, and the pageant in *Love's Labour's Lost*, show the most informal way in which this was done.

It may now be time to summarize *Troelus a Chresyd* so that some treatment of character, situation, style, and versification may be attempted.

Summary.   Rhagddoedydd (the prologue) introduces the play with an explanation of the background of the Trojan war and its cause, the carrying off of Helen from her husband by Paris. Very briefly he outlines the forthcoming action, as Shakespeare does in *Romeo and Juliet*, making no secret of the terrible end. Then he points the moral, the danger of infidelity in love. Calcas[9] is the first character to appear and he comes forward to soliloquize on the difficulty of his own situation, for he fears that Troy will fall to superior Greek force and he does not know what to do. He prepares a sacrifice and prays to Apollo for guidance. Apollo pronounces the doom of Troy. Priaf and his council meet to discuss the possibility of ending the war by handing Helen back to the Greeks, but they decide to keep her.[10] Sinon rushes in to announce the departure to the Greeks of his master Calcas and Cresyd is summoned, for, according to Trojan law, the next of kin is legally responsible for the crime of a fugitive from justice. Cruel judgments on Cresyd are proposed, but the humane recommendations of Hector and Troelus prevail and she is set free. During this trial Troelus falls in love with Cresyd. Troelus now pines in secret, but is overheard by is friend Pandar, who comforts him and encourages him to think he may win Cresyd. Pandar recommends Troelus to Cresyd, who is his niece. She resists the idea of his love at first and then succumbs, accepting Troelus as her servant. Pandar now becomes a kind of chorus, informing us of the bliss of the lovers. Over in the Greek camp Calcas asks for a Trojan prisoner to exchange for Cresyd. The Greeks agree and Diomedes is sent to Troy to arrange the exchange. The Trojan council accepts the offer and Troelus bewails his forthcoming loss of Cresyd. Pandar advises him to forget her and find another love, advice which Troelus scorns.

Troelus and Cresyd now part but arrange to meet in ten nights' time, and Cresyd swears her fidelity. Troelus gives her a ring and a jewel. Diomedes conducts Cresyd back to the Greek camp and at once begins to pay court to her. Troelus is left to complain alone and we hear Cresyd too sighing her regrets towards Troy. Diomedes now wins Cresyd's love. Troelus has a terrible dream, which his sister Cassandra[11] explains as a revelation of Cresyd's infidelity, an interpretation which Troelus violently rejects. Diomedes's cloak is captured in a fray and Troelus sees the jewel he gave Cresyd pinned to it. This is proof of her wantonness. Back in the Grecian camp Diomedes turns suddenly on Cresyd and abuses her as a whore. Cresyd, in despair, throws the blame on the gods for her situation. The gods are incensed and Cupid calls the Planets to pass judgment on Cresyd. A solemn masque of the Planets and the Moon moves about the body of Cresyd, who has fallen senseless. A terrible judgment is pronounced. Cresyd must lose beauty at once and spend the rest of her life a leper amongst beggars outside the walls of Troy. Cresyd awakes from her dream with her beauty gone and bewails her fate. She now sits amongst the leper women and learns how to beg. Troelus passes by from battle, likes the look of Cresyd without recognizing her, throws especially rich alms into her plate and goes on. Cresyd, who has not looked up, asks who the generous knight was. When told it was Troelus, she breaks her heart and dies.

Where did our Welsh author find this material? This great and terrible love story had not previously been told in any form in Welsh. Troy and the Trojan war were known to Welsh writers and are regularly mentioned from the fourteenth century on, but when there is reference to Troelus (and I propose to adhere to the Welsh spellings, except when referring to a specific English version) he is not thought of as a tragic lover but as a fine warrior. There is no mention of the love of Troelus in Dares Phrygius, the main authority on the Trojan war for the medieval Welsh writer. Like Hector, Owain, and Cynan, Troelus is the type of a brave man in Welsh poetry of the fifteenth and sixteenth centuries. Dafydd ap Gwilym does not mention Troelus or Cresyd, but he does refer to the Trojan war and he uses two Trojan ladies, Helen and Policsena, sister of Troelus, for comparison with the beauty of the girl he loves, thus breaking away from the stock Welsh comparisons for beauty, Tegwedd, Nest, Indeg, and the others, and setting a fashion which was to flower later in the work of Tomas Prys, Plas Iolyn.

> Policsena ferch Bria,
> Gwaisg o grair yn gwisgo gra.
> A'r ail fu Ddiodemaf,
> Gwiwbryd goleudraul haul haf.
> Trydedd fun ail Rhun y rhawg
> Fu Elen feinwen fannawg,
> Yr hon a beris cyffro
> A thrin rhwng Gröeg a Thro ... [12]

> (... Polixena, daughter of Priam,
> a comely darling, wearing fur;
> the second was Diodemas,
> fit face of the light-spending sun of summer;
> the third maiden, a second Rhun for the future,
> was the notable, fair, slim Helen,
> she who caused agitation
> and war between Greece and Troy.)

It is the courage of Troelus, not his love, that interests Guto'r Glyn, Gutun Owain, Tudur Aled, and Huw Pennant. But during the 1590s Tomas Prys, Plas Iolyn, spent some time in London, observed the new fashions in narrative verse (e.g. Peele's *Tale of Troy*, Shakespeare's *Venus and Adonis* and *Rape of Lucrece*), and in a *cywydd* to a pretty girl compares her to Venus, Minerva, Diana, Juno, Lucresia, Helen, and Cressida, giving more space to Cressida than to any of the others:

> ... Os teg a fu Gresyt wenn
> a thyner iawn i thonen,
> tegach heb ddim tauogedd
> fy meistres gynes i gwedd ... [13]

(... If fair Cresyd was lovely
and very soft of skin,
lovelier, without churlishness,
is my warm-complexioned mistress.)

And in Cardiff MS 13, of the year 1609, after the phoenix, Venus, Juno, and Pallas have been drawn into service, a poet complains:

rydwy mewn adfyd fel troelws am gresvd ... [14]

(I'm in adversity as Troelus was for Cresyd ...)

It was in London and in English literature that the Welsh dramatist found his inspiration and his material. He was as true a Renaissance man as the Earl of Surrey, Sir Philip Sidney, or Edmund Spenser. Like them he looked at the great literatures of Europe, recognized the deficiencies in the literature of his own country and strove to fill a gap by frank borrowing of material and bold experiment in metrical form. From the English experiments of that time came Shakespeare, Milton, and the whole splendid redirection of English writing. Our Welsh pioneer was beaten by and is only now emerging from the inertia of our stiffening literary traditions.

The author of *Troelus a Chresyd* went mainly to Chaucer and Henryson for his material, and he follows these two poets very closely. He makes no secret of it and indeed claims to have translated the whole work.

O arglwyddes (Cleo) dy bryssur help yr owran
    ym tavod dod rwydddeb i orffen hynn allan
Myvi vy hun am esgusoda wrth gariadddyn aniddic
    nad vy nyfais i mo hynn ond gwaith gwyr dyscedic
A mine er mwyn yr wllys da ytt a ddygais
    ai trois ir iaith Gymraeg yn ore ac i medrais
Am hynn nid wyf yn disgwyl na diolch nac anfodd
    ond dy wyllys da a hynny oth wirfodd
Na vernwch arnaf od wyf ddiffygiol o eirie
    kalyn nessa y gallwyf y dysgedic ir wyf inne ...(p. 62)

(O lady Clio, your active help now;
    give my tongue a fluency to carry this through.
I excuse myself to the unhappy lover,
    that this is not my device but the work of learned men.
And I, for the sake of the good will I bore you,
    have turned it to the Welsh language as well as I was able.

For this I do not expect either thanks or displeasure,
    but your good will and that freely given.
Do not judge me if I am lacking in words;
    I follow the learned ones as closely as I can.)

The author evades the wrath of lovers for having written thus of love
by blaming the story on to the learned writers from whom he translates. Let us not be taken in by this. Chaucer, to whom we owe the
fullness of this love story as a comedy, himself pretended to have done
nothing but translate it into English. Translation conferred authority
on a work in the Middle Ages, just as later the novel, in Daniel Defoe
and Daniel Owen, had to pretend to record real life in order to be
accepted. Here is the corresponding passage in Chaucer's *Troilus and
Criseyde:*

O lady myn, that called art Cleo,
Thow be my speed fro this forth, and my Muse,
To ryme wel this book til I have do;
Me nedeth here noon other art to use.
Forwhi to every lovere I me excuse
That of no sentement I this endite,
But out of Latyn in my tonge it write.

Wherefore I nyl have neither thank ne blame
Of al this werk, but prey yow mekely,
Disblameth me, if any word be lame,
For as myn auctour seyde, so sey I . . . (Bk.II, ll.8-18)[15]

It is easy to see how the Welsh dramatist set about his task; He
sat down first of all to go through Chaucer's poem, selecting passages
for use and keeping, with few exceptions, to the order of events in
Chaucer. Sometimes he translates word for word, at other times he
compresses or expands, where he finds it dramatically necessary. As
he approaches the fifth and last book of Chaucer's *Troilus and Criseyde*
he uses the original more and more freely and on p. 201 of the manuscript his debt to Chaucer ends, apart from a few scraps which he
incorporates into the winding up of the play. In Chaucer the tale
ends, as it does in Shakespeare, with Criseyde's betrayal of the love of
Troilus, and thus is a comedy, strictly speaking, though Hector dies
at the end of Shakespeare's frightening play. It was the Scot, Robert
Henryson, who took the story on to the terrible punishment and
death of Cressida, in his poem *The Testament of Cresseid*, and it was to
Henryson that the Welsh writer went for material to complete his
tragedy.

But just at this point, after putting down Chaucer and before taking up Henryson, the author introduces something for which there is no justification within the play, the sudden and violent attack on Cresyd by her new love, Diomedes. Henryson tells us that Diomedes just got tired of her, fell in love with another girl and sent Cresseid what Henryson calls a Libel of Repudy, excluding her from his presence henceforth. But in Welsh Diomedes storms abruptly on to the stage and without any warning addresses Cresyd thus:

> Ti iw Butten ir Troeaid er moed er penn ith aned
> does ymaith om golwc nad ym byth dy weled
> yr owran y mysc Groegwyr vwyvwy'n puteinia
> o doi di byth lle y bythwy ar kledd hwn ith ladda . . . (p. 202)

> (You've been a whore to the Trojans ever since you were born;
> get out of my sight, let me never see you again,
> now amongst the Greeks prostituting yourself more than ever;
> if you ever come where I am, with this sword I will kill you . . .)

What is the explanation of this accusation and this fury, for if Cresyd can be called a whore, surely Diomedes himself is as much to blame as anyone? Had the author seen Shakespeare's play, in which Thersites refers to Cressida in these terms? Or, and this is more likely, had he seen Heywood's *Iron Age*, in which Sinon, a Greek this time, makes a bet with Diomedes that he will win Cressida's love and succeeds? Possibly the memory of this was in our author's mind, but he neglected to incorporate into his play the motivation for the wrath of Diomedes.

From here on, through the masque of the Seven Planets and their judgment, the Complaint of Cresseid and her death, the Welsh dramatist keeps very close to Henryson, allowing himself some freedom which will be noted later when the translation is discussed. The final fourteen lines, in which the moral of the play is stressed, are suitably indebted to suggestions both from Chaucer and Henryson.

There is no indubitable indication of debt to Shakespeare and even if any debt be established, it can only be one of the slightest kind, though the scene where the council of Troy discusses the future of Helen runs along similar lines in the Welsh play and in Shakespeare. It will be remembered that Shakespeare's play ends with the yielding of Cressida to the love, or lust, of Diomedes, and that the Epistle to the Reader, which prefaces the first quarto edition of Shakespeare's play in 1609, describes it as a witty comedy. Nothing could be further from the Welsh treatment of the tale. There is not a laugh in the whole of *Troelus a Chresyd*, but a unity of mood which is closer to Greek than to English drama.

Most interesting are those scenes in *Troelus a Chresyd* which have no counterpart in any other known version of this story, the appeal of Calcas to Apollo and the trial of Cresyd. Chaucer simply states that Calchas, having consulted the Delphic oracle, has gone over to the Greeks. In the Welsh play we are given, by means of a long soliloquy, a penetrating analysis of the mind of a Quisling. Apollo refuses to advise him but bluntly foretells the fall of Troy, and Calcas is mentally no better off than before. Knowledge of the future only increases our personal responsibility for our actions and worsens our predicament, as the great Greek tragic writers knew. Here are some lines from this impressive scene:

Trwm a rhydrwm yw'r meddwl
   sydd ym kalon mal swmbwl
Nis gad i mi na huno
   nac esmwythdra i beidio . . .
Heb wybod beth sydd oref
   ai mynd ai trigo gartref . . .
Er gwched ydyw Troelus
   a meibion brenin Priamus
Er bod dynion kynn wched
   yn rhef Droya ar a aned
Mae rhai or Groegwyr mor wchion
   ac allef fod o ddynion
A holl gryfdwr y rhyfel
   yn siwr yw'r gyfion avel
Am hynn i mae ynghydwybod
   yn kyhuddo i pechod
Anwiredd yr anghowir
   ai gwagedd a veistrolir
Ac yn y diwaetha
   kyfionder a veistrola
Os aros a rhyfela
   o blaid kenedl Droya
Ac amddiffyn i pechod
   yn erbyn ynghydwybod
Vo ddaw diwrnod or diwedd
   y dygir yn llwyr y dialedd
Pan vytho y tan mor greulon
   yn llosgi Troya dirion

A gwaed gwyr yn aberoedd
  yn llenwi i holl ystrydoedd
Ni cheir amser yno i vyvyr
  beth fydd ore i wneuthur . . .

(Heavy and too heavy is the thought
that is like a goad to my heart;
it does not allow me sleep
nor ease in not doing so . . .
Not knowing what is best,
whether to go or to remain at home . . .
However fine Troelus is,
and the sons of King Priamus,
though there are as fine men
in Troy town as ever were born,
some of the Greeks are as fine
as it is possible for men to be,
and the whole strength of the war
is certainly the hold of righteousness.
Therefore my conscience
accuses their sin;
the untruth of wrongdoers
and their vanity will be mastered
and in the end
righteousness will be master.
If I stay and make war
on the Trojan people's side
and support their sin
against my conscience,
there will come a day in the end
when the fire so cruel
will burn gentle Troy
and men's blood in confluences
will fill all its streets.
There'll be no time then to meditate
on what is best to do . . .)

He now carefully prepares a sacrifice and burns a mixture of frankin-
cense and wormwood in Apollo's honour, calling thus upon the god:

Apolo beth fydd ore
  ai mynd ai trigo gartre
Apolo vo drodd dy atteb
  y lleuad yw gwrthwyneb
A thrwyddod ti Apolo
  yr oedd Syrse yn gweithio . . .

Trwyddod ti y kafodd hevyd
  Medea i holl gyfrwyddyd . . .
Ti a droist yr avonydd
  yngorthwyneb y gelltydd
Ti a wnaethost y mor Apolo
  heb na llenwi na threio . . . (pp. 6-11)

(Apollo, what will be best,
to go or stay at home?
Apollo, your answer turned
the moon to its reverse;
and through you, Apollo,
Circe used to work.
And it was through you
that Medea got her secret knowledge . . .
You turned the rivers
back up against the hillsides;
you made the sea, Apollo,
neither to flow nor ebb . . .)

Whether moved by flattery or aromatic smoke, Apollo gives him his answer and Calcas leaves Troy and his daughter.

The trial of Cresyd for her father's treachery is again to be found only in the Welsh version of this tale. Priaf immediately condemns her to death: the only thing to be decided is the manner of her killing. It is to be noticed that Paris, who has just been pleading for the retention of Helen, is quite heartless when it comes to Cresyd and is the first to suggest a method of putting her to death. Here are some of the proposals:

Paris: Iw llosgi hebryngwch
                am i ffalster ai diffeithwch
              A hynny yw marfolaeth
                kyflownwch y gyfraeth

Eneas: Perwch i thaflu
                i bydew dyfnddu
              Rhy lân yw y llosgi
                am y vath ddrygioni

Antenor: Bwriwch hi heno
                at y llewod ir ogo
              Hi a ymborth am unpryd
                y llewod newynllyd . . . (pp. 27-8)

> (*Paris:*   Lead her off to be burnt
>   for her falsity and vileness;
> and that is death.
>   Carry out the law.
>
> *Eneas:*   Cause her to be thrown
>   into a deep black pit;
> burning is too clean
>   for such wickedness.
>
> *Antenor:*   Throw her tonight
>   to the lions in the cave;
> she would for one meal feed
>   the starving lions . . .)

But Hector and Troelus plead for her and win Priaf's consent to her setting free. Troelus falls in love with her, but does not declare it; Hector promises her his help in any difficulty. All this, so far as can be discovered, is original writing on the part of the Welsh dramatist, though the possibility of dependence on lost scenes from Elizabethan drama cannot be discounted.

    There is originality in his translation too. Let us consider some specimens of how he renders fourteenth-century English and fifteenth-century Scots into Welsh. First of all a close translation where the poverty of psychological terminology in Welsh forces our author to use some English words. This was a fashion of the day and the work of a conservative traditionalist like Wiliam Llŷn bristles with English borrowings. Chaucer, in any case, had taken most of these words from French to enrich the English language. Troelus, in despair after Cresyd's departure, has had bad dreams and seen omens. Pandar, to comfort him, makes light of these and has this to say about the meaning of dreams:

> Dy wendid dy ynfyd-wydd ath drapherthus vreuddwydion
> gad ymaith gida dy holl fyddyliau gweigion
> yrhain sy'n tyfu o felankoli gwydyn
> yr hwnn sydd achos o drafferthus gyntun
>   Hynn yr ydwy yn ei weled
>   nad oes undyn ar a aned
>   a fedr yn union
>   roddi deallt ar vreuddwydion

Yr hên bobl a ddywaid am vreuddwydion
mae'n hwy sy'n dangos dirgelwch duw kyfion
eraill yn doedyd mae o uffernol hudolieth
ac eraill yn meddwl mae komplexiwn amherffaith
    Ar llall sy'n dangos
    mae glothineb yw'r achos
    nis gwyr neb yn sikir
    pwy un or rhain a goelir . . . (p. 178)

(Your weakness, your madness and your troublesome dreams,
let them go with all your empty thoughts;
these grow from a stubborn melancholy,
which causes troublesome slumber.
    This I observe,
    that no man ever born
    can directly
    give a meaning to dreams.

The old people say of dreams
that they show the secrets of a just god;
others that they're from a hellish enchantment,
and others that they're an imperfect complexion.
    And another shows
    that gluttony is the cause.
    No one knows for certain
    which of these is to be believed.)

Here is the counterpart of this in Chaucer. Notice that Chaucer's "prestes of the temple" have become "yr hen bobl" in Welsh:

Thy swevenes ek and al swich fantasie
Drif out, and lat hem faren to meschaunce;
For they procede of thi malencolie,
That doth the fele in slep al this penaunce.
A straw for alle swevenes signifiaunce!
God helpe me so, I counte hem nought a bene!
Ther woot no man aright what dremes mene.

For prestes of the temple tellen this,
That dremes ben the revelaciouns
Of goddes, and as wel they telle, ywis,
That they ben infernals illusiouns;
And leches seyn, that of complexiouns
Proceden they, or fast, or glotonye.
Who woot in soth thus what thei signifie?
            (*Troilus and Criseyde*, V, ll. 358-371)

Sometimes the image is completely altered in translating a line into Welsh. Troilus in Chaucer's poem is bewailing his loneliness now Criseyde has left him and says:

Save a pilowe I fynde naught t'embrace . . .(V, l. 224)

In Welsh this appears as:

Nid oes yma ddim iw weled
ond y llawr y nen ar pared   (p. 174)

(There is nothing here to see
but the floor, ceiling and wall.)

Sometimes the Welshman makes use of a proverbial expression to phrase an idea in a more striking way than the English original. Thus the line

Mote spenden part the remenant for to save   (IV,l.1376)

becomes in Welsh:

ac y treulia swllt yn keissio'r geinioc   (p. 150)

(and spend a shilling seeking the penny.)

Sometimes the image as it occurs in Chaucer is effectively developed in Welsh, as here rather in the manner of the *cywyddwyr*:

Mal rhew yw'r ddyn veindlos
ar eglur leuad gayafnos
tithey yw'r eira oerfeloc
yn toddi wrth eiriesdan gwressoc.   (pp. 41-2)

(Like frost is the slim, pretty girl,
in the clear moon of a winter's night;
you are the chilly snow
melting by a hot, glowing fire.)

The English original runs:

This lady is as frost in wynter moone
and thow fordon, as snow in fire is soone.   (I,ll.524-5)

The Welsh writer's triumph as a translator is his rendering of the lovely and heart-rending ''Complaint of Cresseid'' from Henryson's *Testament*. Here are three stanzas of this sustained lament:

... Ple mae dy ystafell wedy ei gwisco a sidan drosti
mae dy aur vrodiad glustoge ath amrosgo wely
mae'r llysiau gwressoc ar gwinoedd ith gyssuro
ple mae'r kwpane o aur ac arian yn disgleirio
mae dy felys vwydydd ath ddysgle gloywon gwastad
mae dy vlassus seigiau a phob newydd arferiad
ple mae'r dillad gwchion ar mynych ddyfeissie
ple mae'r lawnd ar kamlad ar euraid nodwydde
   hynn i gyd a gefaist
   a kwbwl o hynn a gollaist

Ple mae dy erddi yn llawn o rissiau gwchion
ple mae'r teiau bychein yn llawn o fentyll gwrddion
ple mae'r wastad alay a llysiau wedi ei thrwssio
lle y byddit Mai ac Ebrill arferol i rodio
i gymryd y boregwlith wrth dy blesser ath esmwythdra
ac i wrando ar achwyn y felusbwnk ffilomela
gida llawer glan arglwyddes dan ganu karolau
gen ystlys y gwrddion fentyll ai kyson doriadau
   Hynn a vu ac a ddarfu
pethau eraill rhaid kroessawy

Kymer letty'r klippan am dy eurblas uchelbryd
am dy esmwythglyd wely kymer hynn o wellt oerwlyb
am dy vwydydd gwressoc ar gwinoedd o bell a ddyged
kymer vara toeslyd a sukan sur iw yfed
am dy eglurlais melys ath garole kynn fwyned
kymer oernad gerwin dychryn gen bawb dy glowed
am dy bryd dy wedd dy lendid ath howddgarwch
kymer wyneb gweroc brychlyd yn llawn o ddiffeithwch
   Ac yn lle dy liwt ymarfer
   ar kwpan yma ar klapper ...   (pp. 220-1)

(Where is your bedroom, dressed over with silk;
where are your gold-embroidered pillows and your tumbled bed;
where are the warming herbs and the wine to comfort you;
where are the gold and silver cups sparkling;
where are your sweet foods and your shining, flat dishes;
where are the fine clothes and the many devices;
where's the linen and camlet and the golden needles?
   All this you were given
   and all this you have lost.

Where are your gardens full of fine steps;
where are the little houses full of green mantles;
where is the level alley, decorated with herbs,
where in May and April you used to walk

> to take the morning dew at your pleasure and ease
> and to listen to the plaint of the sweet-songed Philomena,
> with many a lovely lady whilst singing carols
> along the flanks of green mantles with their regular gaps?
> > This was and has ended:
> > other things must be welcomed.
>
> Take the beggar's dwelling for your high-ridged golden mansion;
> for your snug, comfortable bed take this much cold, wet straw;
> for your warming foods and the wine brought from far,
> take doughy bread and sour gruel to drink;
> for your sweet, clear voice and your so gentle carols,
> take a harsh, cold moan that frightens all who hear you;
> for your appearance, your face, your beauty and your
> > attractiveness,
> take a greasy, spotted face full of vileness;
> > and instead of your lute, practise
> > on this cup and clapper.)

What wonderful writing this is! I know of few more frightening lines than

> kymer oernad gerwin dychryn gen bawb dy glowed.

Nor is it all translation, for some of the most effective things in these stanzas are not in Henryson at all. For instance, the charming picture of an Elizabethan garden in lines 2 and 3 of the second stanza quoted above. The level alley with its herbaceous border and the little summer houses are not in the "Complaint of Cresseid". Nor is there any reference to a lute in Henryson, for it was a sixteenth-century instrument and this is a contemporary touch on the part of the Welsh author. Only those Welshmen who had been to the Tudor Court would know what a lute was.

The principal verse forms that occur in *Troelus a Chresyd* have already been exemplified in quotations made for other purposes. For three-quarters of the play, from p. 59 to p. 218 in the manuscript, the metre is the eight-line stanza used by Pandar in his speech on dreams quoted on pp. 100-1 of this essay. The rhyme scheme is aaaabbcc or aaaabbbb. There are four long lines containing four heavy stresses and four short lines with two stresses in each line. The number of syllables varies greatly for this is accentual, not syllabic, metre. Rhagddoedydd usually speaks in long couplets of varying accentual length, with four, five, or even six heavy stresses in a line. Calcas speaks in a short couplet form with an average of seven syllables in a line and two or three heavy stresses. This too is the measure of the scene where Helen's future and Cresyd's fate are debated.

Then towards the end of the play we move into those fine long stanzas in which Cresyd bemoans her lot, but it was not in Henryson that the Welsh writer found this stanza form, for the Scots poem is in the same much shorter rime royal as Chaucer's *Troilus and Criseyde*. Then when Cresyd, now amongst the beggars, has received alms from Troelus and she has been told who he is, she speaks a warning to all lovers in a stanza rather like that of her complaint just quoted, but without the two short lines at the end, a stanza averaging eight lines in length, with the lines all long and a rhyme scheme of couplet rhymes throughout.

A considerable problem faced the dramatist, for no metre existed in Welsh for a work of this length, a dramatic poem of some three thousand lines. The classical twenty-four metres were out of the question, nor was he disposed to accept the newly-evolved English ten-syllable blank verse. For this he can hardly be blamed, for England had a tradition of unrhymed verse, whereas all previous Welsh verse, for at least a thousand years, had been rhymed. His solution was to use rhymed couplets and the stanza forms we have noted, all without *cynghanedd*, and to fit them as well as he could to the different situations of the play. Where the movement of thought is broken or excited, as in the soliloquy of Calcas and the trial of Cresyd, he uses short lines, but for the sustained grief of Cresyd long lines and long stanzas. In between, for most of the action of the play, comes the useful eight-lined stanza, with four long and four short lines. The dialogue does not usually cut across the stanza form, but there are cases where this happens. Altogether he seems to be more indebted to the rime royal of Chaucer and Henryson, though he nowhere reproduces it exactly, than to the free stanzas of his Welsh contemporaries who were breaking away from the traditional shackles.

The solution we get therefore to the metrical problem in drama is the most successful we have had in Welsh before the recent experiments of Mr Saunders Lewis. That accentually equivalent lines may have sometimes ten and sometimes fourteen syllables is an advantage for spoken verse. Syllabic equivalence, unless handled with the mastery of a Racine or broken up by a Shakespeare, can lead to intolerable monotony, whereas lines with an accentual pattern but of varied length allow much wider scope in speech rhythms and give the actor almost as much freedom as run-on blank verse. When this play is acted, therefore, the rhymes do not obtrude and the effect is that of natural speech rhythms just sufficiently tightened for the tense purposes of drama. But the stanza forms, suiting the whole conception of the tragedy, make it more static than Shakespeare's plays and closer to the great tragedies of the Greece.

Should this despised interlude be spoken of thus in the same breath as Shakespeare and Euripides? Though not as great a play in poetry and thought as Shakespeare's *Troylus and Cressida*, it has greater unity. It is the tragedy of Cresyd and there is nothing in *Troelus a Chresyd* which does not bear directly upon her fate. Objection might be made to the second scene of Act i, in which the council of Troy considers what to do about Helen, but this directly concerns Cresyd, for if Helen had been handed back to her husband there would have been no further war and no enforced separation of Troelus and Cresyd. Then the contrast between this consideration of Helen's future and the trial of Cresyd, which follows immediately, is extremely effective and the dramatist is clever enough not to bring Helen to the stage to distract attention from Cresyd, as Shakespeare does. Trial scenes make effective stage material (witness Chinese medieval drama, *The Merchant of Venice*, and the modern crime film), and our author gives us a third trial, that of Cresyd by the gods, before the end of the play.

The main characters in the play are clearly presented and motivated, the analysis of Calcas being particularly interesting and unique in the history of this love story. Could it be that for sixteenth-century Wales this kind of person, who abandons his own country and its interests for a more profitable existence among his country's enemies, had as much topicality as it has had in the Europe of recent decades?

Troelus is a straightforward character, brave and unswervingly faithful. Judged by the conventional idea of a soldier today, he may appear weak, effeminate, and emotional, for we seem to have adopted the English stiff-upper-lipped attitude to emotion. Certainly he is slow to declare his love, he faints and threatens to kill himself, he pines and sighs at great length, but before the end he asserts a desperate nobility in his intention to fight the Greeks until he dies, and a touching magnanimity in the memorial he proposes to erect to Cresyd.

Cresyd is far more complex and here there is a great opportunity for an intelligent and powerful actress. We will never quite agree over Cresyd any more than we do over Hamlet and Falstaff. The unlucky

situations in which she finds herself may be some excuse for her bad
behaviour. She is abandoned by her father and left unprotected in
Troy. Then, when the danger of that situation is lifted, she is torn
from her lover, by her father's plan to regain her, to the alien atmosphere of the Grecian camp. She is the victim of her father's rash and
inconsiderate actions and therefore, in a sense, as much a victim of
fate as was Juliet, so that she may have some cause to upbraid the
gods. But is not her acceptance of Diomedes indecently hurried? She
is even quicker to accept him in the Welsh play than in Chaucer.[16]
We may suspect her of having had a sly eye to the main chance even
in accepting the love of Troelus and the cunning twists of her
proposals for deceiving her father and stealing back to Troy to see
Troelus are indications of a designing nature. One feels that she never
quite loses herself in a situation, but that there is an element of cal-
culation in her most emotional moments. Yet there is sincere
affection and respect for Troelus in her first soliloquy of complaint
towards Troy walls on her first night in the Greek tents, together with
a gloomy half-awareness of the treachery to which she is about to
abandon herself.

From the Elizabethan theatre and quite probably from Shakespeare, who made the most effective use of the device, the Welsh
dramatist learnt the trick of tragic irony. Thus the tragic hero makes a
pronouncement which we know is going to be falsified. This gives us
the pleasant feeling of possessing a knowledge greater than that of the
puppets on the stage and it whets our appetite to see their words made
untrue. Immediately before Shakespeare's Caesar is assassinated he
says:

> But I am constant as the northern star,
> Of whose true-fix'd and resting quality
> There is no fellow in the firmament...
>   (*Julius Caesar*, III.i.57-9)

and we nod our heads in pity and superior knowledge.

Let us see how this device is used in the treatment of Cresyd. In
the scene of her trial in Act i there are several assertions of her
innocence and harmlessness. Hector says:

> Aed honn lle i myned
> ni all hi vawr or niwed   (p. 29)

> (Let her go where she pleases,
> she can do little harm.)

And Troelus pledges his freedom and life as a guarantee of her future good behaviour:

> Rho fy einioes drosti
>   o bu yn honn ddrygioni[17]
> Nac er moed yn arfer
>   a thwyll ne ffalster . . .
> Ac or awr honn allan
>   yr wy vi Troelus vy hunan
> Yn kaethiwo vy rhyddid
>   dros gowirdeb Kressyd.   (p. 34)

> (I'll give my life for her
>   if she was ever wicked,
> or ever familiar with
>   trickery and falsity.
> And henceforth from this hour
>   I Troelus myself pledge
> my freedom for Cresyd's honesty.)

Later, in his first soliloquy expressing his sudden and, he thinks, hopeless love, he compares Cresyd to frost under a clear winter moon (see quotation, p. 102), whereas we know that she will prove an easy wanton. Once more, in the scene where Troelus and Cresyd part, her promise of fidelity is solemn and repeated, she protests too much, and her too rapid surrender to Diomedes is made the more shocking. But a character who is humiliated, or who suffers grievously for his folly or his guilt, ends by becoming sympathetic. So we sympathize with Macbeth in the end and, on another level, with Bertram and Parolles in *All's Well*. No tragic character ever suffered more than Cresyd, nor is there any fall in literature more terrible than hers, suddenly to lose love, beauty and life to atone for infidelity.

Pandar, in the Welsh play, is the type of faithful friend, as he is in Chaucer, and his advice, though worldly and unromantic, is usually sound. He has none of the smirking nastiness of Shakespeare's Pandarus.

There is an alternation in the play between scenes which have one or two characters only and great group scenes. Those scenes, particularly, in which Cresyd is the centre of attention, at her trial by the Trojan council, then by the gods, and at the end when she sits amongst the leprous beggar-women, come powerfully to life upon the stage. How wrong Tatlock was in his criticism of this last scene, in saying that the author missed a dramatic opportunity in not making Cresyd recognize Troelus as he passes by and gives her alms! Recognitions in the last act are the most over-worked trick in drama. Here we have something far more subtle and poignant, the proximity of Troelus and Cresyd without recognition and her final cry of despair and heartbreak when she learns who has just gone by.

It is certainly worth while trying to identify the author of this play. Tatlock's suggestions are not helpful. Mr W.B. Davies thoughtRichard Hughes a possibility. Dic Huws must have seen any number of plays in London and he was an outstanding experimenter in the free meters in Welsh, but there is nothing to suggest any special interest in the theatre on his part, nor is there the least similarity bet-ween the versification of *Troelus a Chresyd* and that of the lyrics of Elizabeth's equerry. Dic Huws could hardly have resisted including an *awdl gywydd* couplet somewhere and there is none in the play. Are there any other possibilities? It is necessary to look for a Welsh writer who was something of a scholar and who was familiar with English literature and with London and the literary fashions of London at the end of the sixteenth and the beginning of the seventeenth century. He must be a North Walian, for *Troelus a Chresyd* is written in a northern dialect of Welsh. In an age when Chaucer was thought difficult and antique[18] and when Henryson was incomprehensible except to Scots, the Welsh writer was at his ease with these authors, and Professor George Thomas, of University College, Cardiff, tells me that the Welsh play helps to explain some difficulties in Henryson's *Testament of Cresseid*.

A not impossible candidate for authorship is Morris Kyffin. He came from near Oswestry and wrote verse in English and Welsh. He knew London well and as Comptroller of Musters knew people like the Earl of Essex, who were interested in drama. His translation of Terence's comedy *Andria* was published in 1588 and he quite prob-ably translated another play by the same author. But Morris Kyffin died in 1598, which is perhaps a little early for him to have been the author of *Troelus a Chresyd*.

Then there was Richard Lloyd, tutor to William Stanley, younger son of the 4th Earl of Derby, a great patron of the drama. Lloyd was at Lathom House in June 1587, when a great cycle of dramatic representations was given. Some plays were performed by the Earl of Leicester's players, and Shakespeare was quite possibly there.[19] Richard Lloyd had published in 1584 *A Briefe Discourse of the most renownded actes and right valiant conquests of those puisant Princes called the Nine Worthies*, under the imprint of R. Warde, London. This is an account of the annual Chester pageant, and Shakespeare made fun of it in *Love's Labour's Lost* (v.2.528-718).

Thomas Hughes, a Cheshire man who published a play called *The Misfortunes of Arthur* in 1587, seems to have been more interested in Ireland than in Wales, and the identity of the author of a play called *Uther Pendragon*, performed by the Admiral's players in 1587, has been lost together with the play. But there is another Welsh writer about whom a good deal is known and who was closely connected with the drama of the age, Hugh Holland, a great traveller, a classical scholar and a poet in English of high reputation in his day. His ability to write Welsh is proved by his *englyn unodl union* amongst the commendatory verses to Coryate's *Crudities* (1611). He wrote a prefatory poem to Ben Jonson's tragedy *Sejanus* (1605) and a sonnet in the first folio of Shakespeare's *Works* (1623), and the presumption therefore is that he knew Shakespeare and Ben Jonson well. He was a member of the Mermaid Club and as a courtier he would realize the possibilities of a masque in the trial of Cresyd by the Planets. The masque was the fashionable entertainment in the Jacobean Court and Shakespeare introduced a masque into his last play, *The Tempest*. Hugh Holland was a Denbigh man and in every way he fits the bill for authorship of *Troelus a Chresyd*, except that there is as yet not the slightest scrap of evidence to tie him to the play. The authorship thus remains an open question, but one well worth pursuit.

The main importance of *Troelus a Chresyd* is that it is the first full-length play, and a tragedy at that, in the Welsh language, and an interesting experiment in versification for drama. But, as Tatlock indicated, it has an interest and an importance for the world outside Wales too, for it comes at the end of the centuries of development of this story in the literatures of Europe and it contributes something new to this development. There is no mention of Cressida, or of any woman whom Troilus loved, in Homer, Dares Phrygius, or Dictys Cretensis. The inventor of this love story is Benoit de Sainte-More in his twelfth-century *Roman de Troie*, where the heroine's name is Briseyde. Guido delle Colonne, in his *Historia Trojana*, helped to popularize Benoit's story without adding much to it, but it is in Boccaccio's *Filostrato* that it is first raised from an incident in the Trojan war to a passionate love story, interesting in its own right. It was Boccaccio who invented the wooing and winning of Criseida, as he names his heroine, and the *Filostrato* was Chaucer's source. In Chaucer's poem Criseyde becomes a complex character, one of the great studies of womanhood in literature. The Welsh writer, depending on Chaucer for the main part of his story, accepted the conventions of courtly love upon which the tale is based. Thus there was nothing reprehensible in a love story which nowhere carries any suggestion of marriage. This is made clear in the terms of Cresyd's acceptance of Troelus as *cavaliere servente*:

> Kroesso wrth wamal naturieth
> mal gwasnaethwr ym gwasanaeth.   (p. 96)

> (Welcome to an unstable nature,
> as a servant into my service.)

Henryson, as we have already seen, gave the tale its tragic conclusion, so that by the end of the fifteenth century it had reached its full growth and was ready for the popularization which the new invention of printing was to give it, in common with the older Trojan material. Caxton had published Chaucer's *Troilus and Criseyde* and his own *Recuyell of the Historyes of Troye* on the Continent a few years before he set up his press at Westminster in 1476. Lydgate's *Troy Book* (written 1412-20) was printed in 1513 and a complete Chaucer was printed by John Kyngston for John Wight at London in 1561, an edition which was used by Thomas Speght for his 1598 and 1602 editions of that poet. George Peele's *The Beginnings, Accidents, and End of the Fall of Troy* was first published in 1589 and eight books of Chapman's translation of Homer's *Iliad* appeared in 1598. At least three plays incorporating the love story of Troilus and Cressida, Heywood's *Iron Age*, the Admiral fragment, and Shakespeare's *Troylus and Cressida*, were being performed about the turn of the century.

For the Elizabethans, Shakespeare, Thomas Heywood, Dekker, and Chettle,[29] the medieval conventions of courtly love were no longer valid. Shakespeare approached the tale through a character of his own invention, the scurrilous Thersites, who sums up the whole action of the play as "lechery, lechery, still wars and lechery; nothing else holds fashion" (*Troilus and Cressida*, V.2.196-7). But there is nothing of this embittered disillusionment in the Welsh handling of the story, which is historically the last sympathetic treatment of these lovers. The Welsh writer's additions to the tale and his handling of it are therefore of especial interest and deserve to be more widely known.

Shakespeare's ruthless treatment killed the story and the ghosts of the medieval Troilus and Cressida did not walk again until 1954, when not only was the Welsh play given its first public performance, but a young Scots dramatist used the story for a television play and a new opera in English was based upon it.

Acknowledgement.   My thanks are due to the Librarian and staff of the National Library of Wales for making Peniarth MS 106 and Mr W. Beynon Davies's thesis on *Troelus a Chresyd* available to me.

Since this essay was written, the following editions of the Peniarth MS 106 text have been published:

Troelus a Chresyd, edited by W. Beynon Davies. Cardiff, University of
Wales Press, 1976.

Troelus a Chresyd, edited and modernised by Gwyn Williams. Llan-
dysul, Gwasg Gomer, 1976.

[1] I have retained the spellings found most often in Peniarth MS 106. Troelys and Troylus occur there once each, Troelws a number of times, but by far the most consistent form is Troelus. Kressyd is consistently used, with the variants Kressyda and Kressida for metrical purposes. Except when quoting from the text I have modernized this to Cresyd. Some spellings which the Welsh writer may have seen in print are the following: Troilus and Creseide, with the variant Creseida, in Wight's *Chaucer* of 1561 and Speght's 1598 and 1602 editions; Troylus and Cressid, the nearest to the Welsh forms, in *Saint Marie Magdalens Conuersion*, I.C. (Joshua Cooke?), London, 1603. Shakespeare's play was entered as *Troilus and Cresseda* in the Stationers' Register, 7 February 1603, but a later entry on 28 January 1609 gives *Troylus and Cressida*, which becomes *Troylus and Cresseida* on the title page of the first quarto of 1609. A later issue in 1609 has Troylus and Cresseid as the spellings. Henslowe's *Diary*, April-May 1559, refers to a *Troylles and Creseda* play to be written by Decker and Chettle.

[2] *Report on Manuscripts in the Welsh Language*, I, Part 2, p. v (1899).

[3] *Report*, I, Part 2, p. 651.

[4] "Examined and partially copied by me, John S. P. Tatlock, University of Michigan, U.S.A., 4 July 1911."

[5] *Le Théâtre Celtique* (Paris 1904), pp. 63-4.

[6] "One of the earliest interlude subjects is *Troelus a Chressyd*, which shows that a tradition of drama had arisen dealing with worldly and fictional stories: that someone had divorced drama from religion and that scores of others had happily followed his example." *Y Ddrama yng Nghymru* (Cyfres Pobun), p. 14.

[7] *Dulliau'r Canu Rhydd* (University of Wales Press, 1952), p. 37.

[8] In the *Report on MSS in the Welsh Language*, J.G. Evans relates this manuscript to Peniarth MS 112, pointing out that by 1619 John Jones had changed his orthography and was using an ingredient in his ink which has corroded the paper. (*Report*, I, Part 2, p. 671). In Peniarth MS 106 a heavy application of ink in the great capitals has caused the paper to disintegrate altogether at some points in the later pages.

[9] Kalkas in the manuscript.

[10] To the war-weary Elizabethans, about the year 1600, the causes of war and the validity of the pursuit of honour as a motive for fighting were serious concerns and are important themes in Shakespeare's *Henry IV*, Part 2, *Henry V, Hamlet*, and *Troylus and Cressida.*

[11] Kassandra in the manuscript.

[12] *Gwaith Dafydd ap Gwilym*, ed. Thomas Parry (University of Wales Press, 1952), p. 137.

[13] Mostyn MS 112, pp. 137-8.

[14] *Canu Rhydd Cynnar*, ed. T.H. Parry-Williams (University of Wales Press, 1932), p. 52.

[15] The text used is that of *The Works of Chaucer*, ed. F.N. Robinson, Oxford University Press.

[16] Cf. MS, p. 172, and Chaucer, *Troilus and Criseyde*, V. ll. 183 ff.

[17] MS, o bu honn un drygioni.

[18] Thomas Speght, who edited Chaucer's *Works* (printed by Adam Islip, London, 1598, and revised ed. 1602), thought it necessary to explain and excuse Chaucer's spelling and grammar, and to defend his versification. He adds, "Moreover, whereas in the explanation of the old words, sundry of their significations by me given, may to some seeme coniectural; yet such as understand the Dialects of our tongue, especially in the North, and have knowledge in some other languages, will iudge otherwise . . .". Speght therefore appends a list of "the old and obscure words in Chaucer explaned", but even this, since it seems likely that our Welsh writer used one of these editions, would not give the author of *Troelus a Chressyd* the full understanding he has of fourteenth- and fifteenth-century English and Scots. In a commendatory letter to Speght's *Chaucer*, Francis Beaumont stresses the difficulty of understanding him, and, after mentioning translations of Petrarch and Ariosto into English, asks, ". . . Shall onely Chaucer our ancient Poet, nothing inferiour to the best amongst all the Poets of the world, remaine alwaies neglected, and never be so well understood of his owne countrie men, as strangers are?"

[19] See A. Keen and R. Lubbock, *The Annotator*, (Putman, 1954), chapter vi.

[20] An entry in Henslowe's *Diary* for April-May 1599 records the advance of five pounds to Dekker and Chettle in earnest of *Troylles and Creseda* for the Admiral's Players.

Black Beauty in Shakespeare

Shakespeare's use of adjectives of skin colour, particularly when applied to Africans, his animadversions on the cosmetic art when applied to white, as opposed to black skins, the warmth of his reference to sunburnt skins, an unfashionable attitude in his day, all this, though dramatised and made to fit a particular person, like everything else in his plays, would appear to reveal an unusual sympathy on the dramatist's part for North African skin colour. Colour adjectives are tricky things to deal with, perhaps because no two persons see exactly the same colours, perhaps simply because words change their meaning over the centuries, and whereas a change of direction in the meaning of such words as charity or revolution or mere might not be perceptible to the ordinary speaker of the language, a change in such common concepts as whiteness and blackness would puzzle anyone. Thus for us to find the word black used to describe red wine or a pretty Englishwoman might come as something of a shock.

As far back as the eleventh century the word black was used to describe a person with black hair or a dark complexion. Later, it was loosely used for non-European races who might be far from black in fact. Thus the late fourteenth century poem *Sir Ferumbras* describes the Saracens as black (1.2785). In Pepys' *Diary* (30 April 1661) we find the lively author speaking of a Mr Hater and his wife and saying, "I found her to be a very pretty, modest, black woman". There is no suggestion that the pretty Mrs Hater was a negress. She was simply black-haired, but otherwise as white as her husband, though of course very few so-called white people are really white.

The words black and Moor came to be used so often together in the sixteenth century that by 1581 we find them fused into the word blackamoor, which passed into common use by late Elizabethan writers. Andrew Boorde, who travelled as far as Jerusalem, in his *Boke of the Introduction of Knowledge*, 1547 (xxxvi 212), reports a man as saying, "I am a blake More borne in Barbary". And he explains,

''There be whyte Mores and black Moors'', meaning that the skin colour of North Africans varies from the comparative fairness or tawniness of the Berbers and Arabs to the pitch blackness of people of the Saharan oases. Purchas' *Pilgrimage*, 1613 (p. 687), distinguishes between the inhabitants of the North African or Barbary coast and those of the Saharan hinterland in speaking of ''The Sea coast Moores, called by a general name Baduini.'' This distinction accords with Boorde's white and black Moors but it was rarely observed once the term blackamoor became indiscriminately used for all the inhabitants of North Africa and the word black became interchangeable with tawny, swarthy, tanned or dark-complexioned. There was little further reference to the Bedouin before the knowledgeable Gibbon and the travellers of the nineteenth century.

Let me consider some examples of this uncertain use of the word black in Shakespeare's work before we come to indubitable blackness. When Gloster in *Richard III* (I.ii.158) calls Clifford black-faced he does not mean that he is a negro. Nor is that the suggestion in the following dialogue in *Two Gentlemen of Verona* (V.ii.8-12), for Thurio is a rather foolish young Italian gentleman and there is no question of his not being ''white''.

> *Thurio:* What says she to my face?
> *Proteus:* She says it is a fair one.
> *Thurio:* Nay then, the wanton lies; my face is black.
> *Proteus:* But pearls are fair; and the old saying is,
>   Black men are pearls in beauteous ladies' eyes.

The ambiguities in the word fair are made use of here and the suggestion is that if gentlemen prefer blondes, women are apt to prefer dark-skinned and dark-haired men.

In *Othello* (II.i.130-132) the phrase ''black and witty'' is used to describe a woman in contrast to ''fair and wise'', black clearly meaning dark-haired or dark-skinned, though of course this playful exchange between Desdemona and Iago carries undertones of awareness of Othello's blackness and of the intermarriage of colour about which the play turns. Shakespeare thinks metaphorically of night as a dark-haired woman, so that we have ''black browed night'' (*MND* III.ii.387) and ''the black brow of night'' (*KJ* V.vi.17), but not necessarily as a negress. *Sonnet 28* has ''swart-complexiond night''. And when death is conceived by Shakespeare as a dark woman the image carries passionate overtones.

... If I must die,
I will encounter darkness as a bride
And hug it in my arms.   (*M for M* III.i.82-4)

The word black came gradually to be limited as a colour adjective to its present day meaning, but there are signs, from the sixteenth century on, that the word swart, which had previously meant black, as in the German *schwarz*, was being used in the looser sense of brown, sunburnt or tawny. In Hylton's *Scala perfeccionis*, 1395 (II.xii), we already find the word swart associated with sunburn, "Beholde me not that I am swart for the sonne hath defaded me". But in the 1533 edition of this work *swart* was replaced by *blacke*. We have already noted Shakespeare's "swart-complexiond night." When Dromio of Syracuse (*Com. of Err.* III.ii.100-101) is asked about the complexion of the kitchen-maid who pursues him, he answers, "Swart, like my shoe." He means not black but the colour of tanned leather, and it is the old process of tanning leather by steeping it in an infusion of oak chips that has given us the words tan, tanned and tawny as colour words for skin that has been much bared to the sun. In 1613 William Browne has a "swart ploughman" (*Britannia*'s *Pastorals* I.iv). Yet Shakespeare uses swarth, a variant of swart, to describe the negroid Aaron in *Titus Andronicus*, "your swarth Cimmerian" (II.iii.72), and the word swarthy for an Ethiop in *Two Gentlemen of Verona* (II.vi.26). Ben Jonson calls Egypt swarthy in *The Poetaster*.

The association of swarthiness of skin with the burning effect of the sun was a commonplace in the sixteenth century and the Prince of Morocco acknowledges this in the first words he speaks in *The Merchant of Venice*,

Mislike me not for my complexion,
The shadow'd livery of the burnisht sun. .   (II.i.1-2)

The Oxford English Dictionary gives the following quotation,

c. 1530: Men of Ethyoppe, that are sonne breent.

Ben Jonson's friend, William Drummond, refers to the "sun-burnt nations of the south" (*Irene* 176) and Middleton in *More Dissemblers Besides Women*, 1623 (V.ii), says of an ill-favoured woman, "She's the sun's masterpiece for tawniness". The adjectives black, swart, swarthy, tawny and sun-burnt could all therefore be used interchangeably for North African skin colour at the time when Shakespeare wrote, and for Welsh skin colour as well. George Owen, writing of certain Welshmen in 1603, says that from the age of ten to twenty-four they spent their lives out of doors watching cattle, which gave their skin a North African darkness. "They seeme more like tawney Moores then people of this lande." (*Description of Pembroke-shire*, V.42).

To provide exotic contrast in the court and country mansion entertainments of the second half of the sixteenth century people were often dressed, disguised and coloured as Moors; at the entertainments given for Queen Elizabeth at Kenilworth in 1575, which may not inconceivably have been seen by the boy Shakespeare, music was provided by a blackamoor orchestra; at a court masque in 1559 there were six Moors dressed in black velvet; and at Lord Unton's wedding in 1580 the torch-bearers were five pairs of cupids, naked children, five black and five white. Shakespeare knew about this faking of blackamoors for purposes of entertainment and he makes Leontes, in *The Winter's Tale*, refer to the practice,

> . . . . But were they false
> As o'erdyed blacks . . .   (I.ii.131-2)

And "o'erdyed blacks" reveals Shakespeare's knowledge that the so-called blackamoor was very often a shade of brown. It was Shakespeare who first brought North Africans seriously and sympathetically into English drama, as persons, that is, not as the black devils of medieval religious drama and this serious treatment of dark-skinned persons in drama was as new and revolutionary a procedure as the later adoption of the peasant or worker as a possible hero of fiction. For it is striking that all Shakespeare's black dramatic persons are in some way admirable.

We meet Shakespeare's first North African in *Titus Andronicus*, one of his first experiments in tragic writing. Aaron the Moor is the follower and lover of the blonde Tamora, Queen of the Goths. (Later, in *Othello*, he was to give us another study in almost absolute evil in the person of Iago, loosely repeating the Titus Andronicus-Aaron pattern in the Othello-Iago, but with the skin colour reversed, the Moor now noble and the Italian vicious.) In his first speeches Aaron makes clear to us his proud, lustful, scheming nature. Nor is his colour left in any doubt. He refers to his own "fleece of wooly hair", Bassanius calls him a "swarth Cimmerian", Lavinia talks of Tamora's "raven-coloured love" (all in II.iii.24-84), and when Aaron brings good news, Titus Andronicus exclaims,

> Did ever raven sing so like a lark?   (III.i.159)

In the tradition of the old religious plays, Aaron's colour accords with his character and, in his contempt for the truthfulness of Titus, he himself sums the matter up.

> Let fools do good and fair men call for grace,
> Aaron will have his soul black like his face.   (III.i.205-6)

In the next scene there is talk of . . .

>   . . . a black ill-favoured fly
> Like to the empress' Moor . . .

and

>   . . . . a fly
> That comes in likeness of a coal-black Moor.

No doubt is left in our minds that Aaron is a "black", not a "white" Moor.

It may surprise us, since this is so, that Shakespeare makes Aaron defend his colour in a convincing and admirable way. When Tamora has a child by Aaron and it turns out to be black, the Nurse, following the old tradition, calls it a devil.

> A joyless, dismal, black and sorrowful issue:
> Here is the babe, as loathsome as a toad
> Amongst the fairest breeders of our clime:
> The empress sends it thee, thy stamp, thy seal,
> And bids thee christen it with thy dagger's point.   (IV.ii.70-3)

This is the point at which we begin to feel sympathy for the otherwise repellent Aaron. He cries out, "Is black so base a hue?" and we must admire the pride and spirit with which he prepares to defend his son.

As part of this racial confrontation there occur two very interesting ideas connected with black skin, first that it is superior to white skin in not betraying the secrets of the heart with blushing, and second that it requires no artificial colouring to enhance its beauty, ideas to which Shakespeare was to return in other works, thus showing that they were of especial interest to him. Aaron faces up with anger and contempt to Tamora's two grown-up white sons, who threaten to kill the newborn child.

> Ye white-limed walls! ye alehouse painted sings!
> Coal-black is better than another hue
> In that it scorns to bear another hue;
> For all the water in the ocean
> Can never turn the swan's black legs to white,
> Although she lave them hourly in the flood. (IV.ii.99-104)

Then, a little later, when Chiron exclaims,

> I blush to think upon this ignomy . . .

Aaron counters scornfully,

> Why, there's the privilege your beauty bears:
> Fie, treacherous hue, that will betray with blushing
> The close enacts and counsels of the heart!
> Here's a young lad framed of another leer.
> Look, how the black slave smiles upon his father,
> As who should say, "Old lad, I am thine own."

To guarantee her silence Aaron suddenly kills the Nurse and compares the deed to the killing of a pig. He already has a plan. A friend and fellow-countryman of his is married to a European woman who also has just borne a child, but in this case the child is as white as the mother. Muliteus will be persuaded to relinquish the child, which will be taken to Titus Andronicus as his child by Tamora. It will become the emperor's heir, whilst Aaron will bring up his own dark child secretly. As he carries off the baby, he says,

> Come on, you thick-lipt slave, I'll bear you hence;
> For it is you that puts us to our shifts.
> I'll make you feed on berries and on roots,
> And feed on curds and whey, and suck the goat,
> And cabin in a cave, and bring you up
> To be a warrior and command a camp.   (IV.ii.175-180)

Thinking forward into Shakespeare's later work it is difficult not to see here a sketch of the infancy and upbringing of Othello. (Shakespeare rather similarly uses the device of the childhood of a son to throw light on the nature of Coriolanus.)

The crying of the child betrays Aaron as he conceals it in a ruined building and tries to still it. "Peace, tawny slave". Is he here attempting to lighten the darkness of his offspring, or is this another case of the loose equivalence of black and tawny? Aaron is brought before the triumphing Lucius and manages to save his son's life by confessing his own misdeeds. A Goth, listening to the recital, exclaims,

> What, canst thou say all this and never blush?   (V.i.121)

So Aaron goes, proud and unrepentant, to a terrible death.

Shakespeare returns to the commendation of dark skin and to the idea that it does not require cosmetic colouring, in *Love's Labour's Lost*. There seems to be no dramatic necessity for this, since Rosaline, the girl in question, is not a negress, nor even a black or a white Moor. Berowne commends a letter "to her white hand" and, in his disgust with himself for having fallen in love, he describes her as,

> A whitely wanton with a velvet brow,
> With two pitch-balls stuck in her face for eyes.   (III.i.193-4)

The word pitch sticks in his mind and a little later we overhear him complaining again about being in love. "I am toiling in a pitch, pitch that defiles: defile! a foul word". (IV.iii.2-3) The King makes matters worse by comparing Rosaline to another black substance:

> By heaven, thy love is black as ebony.

Berowne now switches to the defence of her colour and the argument passes beyond hair colour to the whole complexion.

> Is ebony like her? O wood divine!
> A wife of such wood were felicity.
> O who can give an oath? Where is a book?
>   That I may swear beauty doth beauty lack,
> If that she learn not of her eye to look:
>   No face is fair that is not full so black.   (IV.iii.244-250)

The King replies with a medieval association, a platitude and a contemporary allusion.

> O paradox! Black is the badge of hell,
> The hue of dungeons and the school of night.

Now follows an attack on the whole of the fashion for fairness in woman, a fashion sealed in that day by an unmarried, fair-haired, fair-skinned queen, when even to be sunburnt was unfashionable. (Aeneas, in *Troilus and Cressida*, makes a courtier's judgement when he says,

> The Grecian dames are sunburnt and not worth
> The splinter of a lance.   (I.iii.282-3))

Berowne protests against the King's dismissal of blackness.

> O, if in black my lady's brows be deckt,
>   It mourns that painting and usurping hair
> Should ravish doters with a fair aspect;
>   And therefore is she born to make black fair.
> Her favour turns the fashion of the days,
>   For native blood is counted painting now;
> And therefore red, that would avoid dispraise,
>   Paints itself black to imitate her brow.

This pronouncement calls forth a chorus of quick-fire mockery.

> *Dumaine:*   To look like her are chimney-sweepers black.
> *Longaville:* And since her time are colliers counted bright.
> *King:*   And Ethioppes of their sweet complexion crack.
> *Dumaine:*   Dark needs no candles now, for dark is light.

Far from being beaten by these stinging paradoxes, Berowne still has a telling shot in his locker, the natural permanence of dark colour in contrast to the ephemeral quality of cosmetics applied to fair skin.

> Your mistresses dare never come in rain
>   For fear their colours should be washt away

Thus Shakespeare develops an idea which first occurred to him in the creation of Aaron.

In yet another early play, *A Midsummer Night's Dream*, there occurs another dark-skinned boy, Indian this time, not African, who must have been given charming prominence in the train of Titania, the Fairy Queen, though, since he is given no words to speak, he does not appear in the list of persons in the play. This boy is the subject of the quarrel between Titania and Oberon, which results in all the amusing and dangerous confusions of the plot, and Titania talks about him and his Indian mother with much warmth and poetry.

> The fairy land buys not the child of me.
> His mother was a votress of my order,
> And, in the spiced Indian air, by night,
> Full often hath she gossip by my side,
> And sat with me on Neptune's yellow sands,
> Marking th'embarked traders on the flood;
> When we have laughed to see the sails conceive
> And grow big-bellied with the wanton wind;
> Which she, with pretty and with swimming gait
> Following, her womb then rich with my young squire,

Would imitate, and sail upon the land,
To fetch me trifles and return again
As from a voyage, rich with merchandise.
But she being mortal, of that boy did die;
And for her sake do I rear up her boy;
And for her sake I will not part with him.   (II.i.123-138)

So we have another case of reluctance to give up a dark-skinned child, and evidence of Shakespeare's continuing and sympathetic interest in dark skin colour, especially when it is naturally dark and not induced by dyeing.

The proud, warlike and dignified Prince of Morocco, in *The Merchant of Venice*, is the first really likeable North African in Shakespeare's work. A stage direction in the First Quarto refers to him as a Tawny Moor and when a flourish of cornets has announced him into Portia's presence his first act of courtship is a proud ,and poetic defence of his colour.

Mislike me not for my complexion,
The shadow'd livery of the burnisht sun,
To whom I am a neighbour and near bred.
Bring me the fairest creature northward born,
Where Phoebus' fire scarce thaws the icicles,
And let us make incision for your love
To prove whose blood is reddest, his or mine.
I tell thee, lady, this aspect of mine
Hath fear'd the valiant: by my love, I swear
The best-regarded virgins of our clime
Hath loved it too: I would not change this hue,
Except to steal your thoughts, my gentle queen.   (II.i.1-12)

He claims to be servant and neighbour and cousin to the sun, and is full of scorn for those whose skin and blood are not warmed by it. Portia is impressed but tells him that her father's will prevents her from making her own choice of a husband. But for that, she says,

Yourself, renowned prince, then stood as fair
As any comer I have lookt on yet
For my affection.

"As fair as any comer". What a charming remark to make to a dark-skinned man. Shakespeare rarely misses an opportunity of playing upon the ambiguities of the word *fair* and its implied antitheses, and Morocco must surely be pleased that Portia should pay him the compliment of this word.

He is now brought face to face with the three caskets and the fateful choice, and after what he has said about himself we are not surprised to find this neighbour of the sun veering towards the sunny metal, gold. His defence of his choice is noble and worthy of Portia, but he chooses the wrong casket, takes his luck stoically and departs with a heavy heart. Her gentle comment is, "A gentle riddance". Of course, she is not sorry, for now the chances are that her future husband will be a man of her own colour, and Bassanio is already in her mind, if not her heart. So, before leaving the stage, she expresses the hope,

> Let all of his complexion choose me so.

Her next suitor, the white Prince of Aragon, is dismissed with much more contempt when he in turn has failed to guess aright.

> Thus hath the candle singed the moth.
> O, these deliberate fools! (II.viii.79-80)

We come now to the central study, for which Aaron and Morocco were sketches, *Othello*, with a North African, for the first time, as tragic hero, a study in Mediterranean psychology, in the contrast between Machiavellian coldness and hot blood, passion and quickness to jealousy. It is clear that Othello is very dark, not just tawny in our present meaning of the word. Roderigo calls him "thick lips" and Iago refers to him as "an old black ram". Brabantio, Desdemona's father, calls him a "foul thief" (note the opposition to fair) and asks,

> Whether a maid so tender, fair and happy,
> So opposite to marriage that she shunn'd
> The wealthy curled darlings of our nation,
> Would ever have, t'incur a general mock,
> Run from her guardage to the sooty bosom
> Of such a thing as though . . .   (I.ii.71-6)

The father's incredulity is answered by Othello's account of his wooing, which convinces everyone that he used no African witchcraft, and the Duke's comment is,

> I think this tale would win my daughter too.   (I.iii.171)

But when Iago contrives to sow the dreadful seeds of suspicion in Othello's mind that Desdemona is unfaithful to him, Othello is ready to put the blame for this on his colour, his lack of courtly graces and his age, but first of all his colour.

> ... Haply, for I am black,
> And have not those soft parts of conversation
> That chamberers have; or for I am declined
> Into the vale of years ...   (III.iii.203-6)

The story moves to its terrible conclusion, Iago's intrigue succeeds, Othello kills Desdemona and then learns the truth. Iago goes to his punishment with the stoicism of Aaron the Moor, but Othello, before killing imself, weeps unaccustomed tears and pathetically associates his folly and his loss once more with the difference in colour, for he asks Lodovico, in his report on the affair, to speak of him as he is,

> ... of one whose hand,
> Like the base Indian, threw a pearl away
> Richer than all his tribe ...   (V.ii.347-9)

The final comment on the Moor is that of Cassio,

> For he was great of heart.

We have seen greatness of heart and passionate love lead to murderous jealousy, in the person of a North African, a Moor, and we can now see what might perhaps have happened if the Prince of Morocco had picked the right casket and there had been someone like Iago in his entourage. But I come near to the grave but sometimes tempting error of imagining what might have happened before or after the play. Better to take the misfortune of Othello as unique and the Prince of Morocco as bounded by and existing only in *The Merchant of Venice*.

Shakespeare was soon to write another tragic play set around the Mediterranean and in North Africa, and if Othello was a dark, black Moor, Cleopatra, for Shakespeare, was a white Moor, a tawny. The Ptolemies, of course, were Greeks, but Shakespeare shows no interest in, or even awareness of, this fact. For him Cleopatra was a North African queen, tawny, passionate, a gipsy. Ordinary men cannot understand Antony's love for her, any more than they could Desdemona's love for Othello. The very first words of *Antony and Cleopatra* stress this and indicate what kind of Cleopatra we are to expect, certainly not the ''whitely wanton'' who too often appears on the modern stage.

> Nay, but this dotage of our general's
> O'erflows the measure: those his goodly eyes,
> That o'er the files and musters of the war
> Have glow'd like plated Mars, now bend, now turn

> The office and devotion of their view
> Upon a tawny front: his captain's heart
> Which in the scuffles of great fights hath burst
> The buckles on his breast, reneges all temper,
> And is become the bellows and the fan
> To cool a gipsy's lust.

Yet this is the love which Shakespeare is to glorify with some of his finest poetry.

When Antony is away and Cleopatra fears that he does not love her any more, she is ready, as Othello had been, to put the blame on her colour and her age. (She could never accuse herself of lack of the courtly arts.) She wonders whether he will

> . . . think on me,
> That am with Phoebus' amorous pinches black
> And wrinkled deep in time?   (I.v.31-3)

If for the Prince of Morocco the sun was a neighbour and a cousin, for Cleopatra it is a lover, and her swarthy colour is the result of the bruises left by its playful and loving pinches. "With Phoebus' amorous pinches black" is the feminine counterpart of "The shadow'd livery of the burnish't sun", the associations of physical love replacing those of warfare in North African sunshine. But even though in her momentary self-despising mood Cleopatra calls herself black, we should think of her as tawny, of the colour of old bruises, black in the broad Elizabethan sense.

Enobarbus tells us that he once saw Cleopatra "hop forty paces through the public street". (II.ii.237) Gipsies were known to the Elizabethans as dancers in the street and in a journal written in 1605, not long before Shakespeare wrote *Antony and Cleopatra*, the Earl of Nottingham speaks of "Gypsies, men and women, da_uncing and tumbling much after the Morisco fashion" (O.E.D. morisco). Morisco dancing, morris dancing, Morocco, gipsy, Egyptian, these associations are all implicit in Enobarbus's report. And once more the old fair-foul opposition and ambiguities are here and give point to Antony's bitter cry,

> This foul Egyptian hath betrayed me.   (IV.xii.10)

In his anger it seems to him that she has behaved "like a right gipsy", but a little later, as he dies in her arms, all is at last well between them. If the Prince of Morocco and Othello were for Shakespeare the type of North African manhood, then Cleopatra was North African

woman, and Shakespeare's Cleopatra is surely the finest study we
have of passionate womanhood.

Shakespeare's interest in North Africans and in their skin colour
has reached its peak in two great plays which deal with North African
manhood and womanhood in their most characteristic moods. He is
reaching the end of his career as a dramatist but he has yet one more
marriage between a North African and a fair European to give us, a
marriage which in a sense is peripheral to the plot but which, like the
quarrel over the little Indian boy in *MND*, is the ultimate source of
the action. *The Tempest* begins with the wreck of the ship which carries
the King of Naples and his courtiers back from Tunis, where they
have been celebrating the wedding of Claribel (and what name could
more suggest fairness) to the King of Tunis. As in *Othello* there are
some who disapprove of this kind of match, and Sebastian bluntly
blames the King for the predicament in which they find themselves.

> Sir, you may thank yourself for this great loss,
> That would not bless our Europe with your daughter,
> But rather loose her to an African . . .   (II.i.122-4)

(You loose a mare into a field with a stallion when you wish to breed
from her. This cynical reduction of human behaviour to an animal
level reminds us of Iago's view of the love between Desdemona and
Othello,

> . . . an old black ram
> Is tupping your white ewe.)

Except for the distance that separates Tunis and Naples the King has
until now seen nothing wrong in the marriage, and Gonzalo, as
though defending it by referring to an ancient love story associated
with Tunis, harks back to the famous affair between Aeneas and
Dido, Queen of Carthage.

We have observed continuous signs in the plays of
Shakespeare's interest in and sympathy for tawny skin and actually
black persons, and in the fair-foul opposition which sprang from this
interest, so we may reasonably look for similar signs in his non-
dramatic poems, particularly in the Sonnets, which are partly auto-
biographical and which must have been written over a number of
years when he was writing for theatre. There is much reference in the
Sonnets to the black beauty of a woman, who is usually contrasted
with Shakespeare's fair male friend, her foulness, in more than one
sense, in strife with his fairness. Once more the warning must be

given that her ''blackness'' may be taken to be no more than tawniness, accompanied by black eyes and hair, until one unmistakably
sees a negress in the description.

The Sonnets, too, show Shakespeare's detestation of cosmetics.
(This dislike, dramatised, is most central in *Hamlet*, where Hamlet,
pondering his own hesitations, concludes,

> And thus the native hue of resolution
> Is sicklied o'er with the pale cast of thought.   (III.i.85-6)

I take cast here to mean plaster cast. Shakespeare has observed that
the feminine process of making up sometimes involves the application
of plaster to the face and neck to cover wrinkles and to act as a foun-
dation for the application of colour. Elizabethan women plastered
heavily, the Queen as much as any. Claudius, in Act III sc. i,
compares his guilt to

> The harlot's cheek, beautied with plastering art.

He has observed the thickness of plaster sometimes required, and so
has Hamlet, for he says to the skull, ''Now get you to my lady's
chamber, and tell her, let her paint an inch thick, to this favour she
must come.'' Hamlet's interest in cosmetics runs through the whole
play and is clearly related to his disillusionment with the world and its
appearances. Through poor Ophelia, though he must be thinking of
his mother at the same time, he accuses the whole of the sex. ''I have
heard of your paintings too, well enough; God gave you one face, and
you make yourselves another''. (III.i.144-5) For Hamlet the whole
practice of cosmetics has assumed a metaphorical significance. Con-
templation seems to him, at a time when action is required, to have
the falseness of harlotry. His musings are as worthless as a
courtesan's oaths. Thought corrupts action, just as plastering and
painting corrupt the natural looks, ''the native hue''. This is a great
original metaphor and it links two of the main sources of Hamlet's
disgust, the falsity of female beauty and his own trick of overmuch
thinking. Surely he must once have seen the face of a woman he knew
''sicklied o'er with the pale cast'' before colour was put on.)

In the Sonnets it is the fair friend who requires no painting,
which is here used metaphorically for flattery.

> I never saw that you did painting need,
> And therefore to your fair no painting set.   (83)

Shakespeare speaks of ''false painting'' (67) and calls artificial aids to beauty the "bastard signs of fair" (68). Again using it as a metaphor for flattery, he writes,

> And their gross painting might be better used
> Where cheeks need blood . . .   (82)

It is later in the generally accepted order of the Sonnets that references to blackness appear, for even as late as Sonnet 115 it is time, not the sun, which tans sacred beauty. The change comes with Sonnet 127, the first written to the dark woman, whoever she may have been.

> In the old age black was not counted fair,
> Or if it were, it bore not beauty's name;
> But now is black beauty's successive heir . . .

In Sonnet 130 Shakespeare speaks of the woman with whom he is in love with realistic astonishment.

> If snow be white, why then her breasts are dun;
> If hairs be wires, black wires grow on her head.

Black wiry hair, dun breasts, surely these epithets could only apply to a black woman. She is certainly no fair-skinned, pink-and-white beauty, for he goes on to say,

> I have seen roses damaskt, red and white,
> But no such roses see I in her cheeks.

In the next sonnet, 131, he tells her,

> Thy black is fairest in my judgment's place.

And Sonnet 132 ends thus,

> Then will I swear Beauty herself is black,
> And all they foul that thy complexion lack.

So it is not a matter just of hair and eyes, it is a matter of complexion. But a terrible disillusionment follows a betrayal, the nature of which is not difficult to imagine from what the Sonnets tell us. Shakespeare regrets the lack of judgement which has led him

> To put fair truth upon so foul a face.

He makes the situation as clear as is possible in Sonnet 144, which begins,

> Two loves I have of comfort and despair . . .

In his eyes she has now become "a woman colour'd ill" and he speaks of her "foul pride". In Sonnet 147 he is "past cure" and "frantic-mad".

> My thoughts and my discourse as madmen's are,
> At random from the truth vainly exprest;
> For I have sworn thee fair, and thought thee bright,
> Who art as black as hell, as dark as night.

Once more he blames his eyes for their false vision.

> O me, what eyes hath Love put in my head,
> Which have no correspondence with true sight ... (148)

He begins to wonder whether the opinion of everyone around him is right after all, and whether he is wrong in loving a woman of such unconventional colour in Elizabethan London.

> If that be fair on which my false eyes dote,
> What means the world to say it is not so?   (148)

Sonnet 152, the last in the sequence written to the dark woman, ends with these bitter words,

> For I have sworn thee fair; more perjured I
> To swear against the truth so foul a lie.

So fairness and foulness are once more presented in ambivalent opposition. Shakespeare has revealed to us the source of this telling contrast of fair and foul, a contrast which he was to remove from the personal experience of love to make one of the basic thought patterns of his writing, nowhere more impressively than in *Macbeth*.

There may be no need to relate Shakespeare's experience with the dark woman of the Sonnets to his continued interest in North Africans and their skin colour, though the "dun breasts" and "black wires" of Sonnet 130 are significant pointers. Many "whitely wantons" with black hair and eyebrows have been put forward as the dark lady of the Sonnets, in the critics' reluctance to accept a negress, but my favourite is G.B. Harrison's suggestion, a black girl called Lucy Negro, who took part in the Inns of Court revels in 1594, an entertainment in which the Earl of Southampton, friend and patron of Shakespeare if not the "fair friend" of the Sonnets, was involved. Certainly the bitter disappointment with which that love ended did nothing to impair Shakespeare's sympathy with dark-skinned persons in his dramatic writing. From the very beginning to the end of his career the interest and sympathy are there. Shakespeare is unique in English in the number of love affairs and marriages between North Africans and Europeans which he puts into his plays.

The Loneliness of the Homosexual in Shakespeare

The love relationship is central to much of Shakespeare's work and he has given us some famous pairs of lovers. There are consummations that please everyone, but in some cases love leads to death. In others it seems fortuitous, so that so long as Jack gets his Jill it does not matter who Jill is. In *Midsummer Night's Dream* it can be decided by flower juice dropped in the eyes; in *The Two Noble Kinsmen* it is decided by the gods; in *The Merchant of Venice* it depends on the choice of the right casket, though there some judgement is involved. Sometimes there is conflict, which may continue after marriage, as in *The Shrew* and *Much Ado*. The love bond may be warped by hideous jealousy, as in *Othello* and *The Winter's Tale*, or by suspicion, as with Hamlet and Ophelia. Sometimes one partner dominates, and this can be the woman, as with Helena and Bertram, Portia and Bassanio.

I have referred to cases of heterosexual love, but Shakespeare knew that there could be passion outside this bond, which is usually thought of as normal. He knew it could exist between members of the same sex; he accepted this, sympathised with it and fitted it into his patterns of human relationship. In the *Sonnets* the triangular relationship of poet, friend and mistress is clearly presented. Up to a point there is growing passion in his references to the friend, but *Sonnet XX* (in the usual order) makes it clear that a physical side to this love is out of the question.

> A woman's face, with Nature's own hand painted,
> Hast thou, the master-mistress of my passion . . .
> And for a woman wert thou first created;
> Till Nature, as she wrought thee, fell a-doting,
> And by addition me of thee defeated,
> By adding one thing, to my purpose nothing.
>> But since she prickt thee out for women's pleasure,
>> Mine be thy love, and thy love's use their treasure.

Pricking out is the chance selection of a name by sticking a pin
through paper, but in a pun, and not the only time Shakespeare puns
on the word, the poet refers to the physical characteristic which made
physical love between them impossible for him.

It could have been this nearness to a homosexual experience,
coupled with acquaintanceship with homosexuals, which gave Shakespeare the sympathy he shows for them in his works. Where then is
this sympathy to be observed in the plays? *Twelfth Night* is a study of
different kinds of love, but the love of Antonio for Sebastian is not
often noticed in criticism or allowed to become obvious on the stage.
Let us consider the language Shakespeare gives to this sea captain,
who has appointed himself guide and counsellor to his inexperienced
young friend, having saved him from drowning. Sebastian's instinct
is to venture forth alone to explore this strange city, but this makes
Antonio sad, whilst at the same time he is genuinely worried about
Sebastian's safety. He says,

> If you will not murder me for my love, let me be your
> servant.   (II.i.36-7)

Antonio has enemies at the court of Orsino and it is he who is really in
danger.

> But come what may, I do adore thee so
> That danger shall seem sport, and I will go.   (II.i.48-9)

Later, when followed by Antonio, Sebastian accepts his company.

> I will no further chide you. (III.iii.3)

Antonio replies,

> I could not stay behind you: my desire,
> More sharp than filed steel, did spur me forth;
> And not all love to see you, though so much
> As might have drawn me to a longer voyage,
> But jealousy what might befall your travel,
> Being skilless in these parts; which to a stranger,
> Unguided and unfriended often prove
> Rough and unhospitable: my willing love
> The rather by these arguments of fear
> Set forth in your pursuit.   (III.iii.4-13)

At this point Antonio seems embarrassed by his devotion to Sebastian
and tries to show that he is motivated more by concern for the young
man's safety than by love, but the words love, desire and jealousy

interpose. Sebastian too is embarrassed by his temporary inability to reward this care.

> . . . My kind Antonio,
> I can no other answer make but thanks
> And thanks and ever; oft good turns
> Are shuffled off with such uncurrent pay:
> But were my worth, as is my conscience, firm,
> You should find better dealing.   (III.iii.14-19)

There is no suggestion of reciprocated love in this statement, only a friendly gratitude which could take the form of patronage or some token payment, were Sebastian back home in his usual situation. Nor is there any sign that he understands the nature of Antonio's passion.

Later, when they have gone different ways, Antonio comes to the rescue of Viola, whom he takes to be Sebastian, from Sir Toby Belch. Sir Toby asks,

> You sir! why, what are you?   (III.iv.317)

Antonio answers,

> One, sir, that for his love dares yet do more . . .

When Viola, dressed as Cesario, denies all knowledge of Antonio, the outraged sea captain protests to the officers,

> Let me speak a little. This youth that you see here
> I snatched one half out of the jaws of death,
> Relieved him with such sanctity of love,
> And to his image, which methought did promise
> Most venerable worth, did I devotion.   (III.iv.359-363)

In the last act Antonio faces his enemy, Orsino, and boldly flings back the accusation of thief and pirate.

> Antonio never yet was thief or pirate,
> Though, I confess, on base and ground enough
> Orsino's enemy. A witchcraft drew me hither:
> That most ungrateful boy there at your side
> From the rude sea's enraged and foaming mouth
> Did I redeem; a wreck past hope he was:
> His life I gave him, and did thereto add
> My love, without retention or restraint,
> All in his dedication; for his sake
> Did I expose myself, pure for his love
> Into the danger of this adverse town . . .   (V.i.72-82)

The language of this brave sea captain is throughout the language of passion where Sebastian is concerned.

Viola and her brother are reunited and all the absurd complications will be explained. Olivia is content to switch from Cesario to Sebastian and the latter is as happy to accept a lady he has never seen before but who invites him to her splendid house and quickly arranges to marry him. After expressing amazement at the likeness between brother and sister, poor Antonio stands aside in silence for the rest of the scene, for there is nothing in all this for him. Viola's situation is explained and Olivia's surprise has more joy in it, for it gives her a satisfactory husband. So the conventional pairing off takes place. Malvolio has thundered off in righteous anger, but Antonio retires to the periphery of the happy company, despondent and speechless.

Another Antonio, this time in *The Merchant of Venice*, suffers a somewhat similar experience, though he is more restrained in the expression of affection for Bassanio, whose name is curiously like Sebastian's. When the play opens, this Antonio, who is the merchant of Venice of the title, suffers from an unexplained melancholy. He denies concern about his ships at sea and exclaims, "Fie! Fie!" when it is suggested that he is in love, a notable cause in literature of melancholy, as though there is something revolting in the idea. When alone with Bassanio his first words, showing what is on his mind, are,

> Well, tell me now, what lady is the same
> To whom you swore a secret pilgrimage ... (I.i.119-120)

Bassanio shows some shame for the way he has squandered his own estate and misused money previously borrowed from Antonio. Now he would like to borrow more money, for a venture which will restore his finances and enable him to repay Antonio, that is the courtship of Portia at Belmont. Portia, he says, has given him silent encouragement, "fair speechless messages", so that this is likely to be a sound investment. He now makes her wealth the first consideration in his plea to Antonio, whatever his private feelings are, but he makes the point that she is also fair and virtuous.

> In Belmont is a lady richly left;
> And she is fair, and, fairer than that word,
> Of wondrous virtues ... (I.i.160-2)

Antonio's money is for the moment all tied up in ventures abroad but he briefly tells Bassanio to borrow what money he can on Antonio's credit in Venice. It is a bitter and ironical situation for Antonio, and cause enough for melancholy, for because of this, and the contract with Shylock, he is in a fair way to losing his young friend and protégé, his money and his life. Apart from his meeting with Shylock, and the trial scene in Act IV scene i, Antonio is kept in the background, but when, during the trial, he prepares his mind for apparently inevitable death, he makes a revealing statement about himself.

> I am a tainted wether of the flock,
> Meetest for death: the weakest kind of fruit
> Drops earliest to the ground; and so let me.
> You cannot better be employed, Bassanio,
> Than to live still, and write mine epitaph.   (IV.i.115-9)

Antonio of Venice may not have been familiar with sheep, but Shakespeare of Stratford was, and a wether is a castrated ram, not good enough to keep as a ram for breeding and therefore made unable to do so and expendable to the farmer. Antonio is aware of something in his nature which makes him unable to breed and therefore he too is expendable to human society and fit for the slaughter. As for breeding, the lovers will soon fall to it once he is gone. Like Hamlet, his only hope is for a friend to speak well of him when he is dead. Then he commends himself to Bassanio's new wife, whom he thinks he has not met, not knowing yet that she is the learned doctor of law.

> Commend me to your honourable wife,
> Tell her the process of Antonio's end;
> Say how I loved you, speak me fair in death,
> And, when the tale is told, bid her be judge
> Whether Bassanio had not once a love.   (IV.i.273-7)

There is some comfort for him in Bassanio's claim that he would sacrifice wife and all to save Antonio. Gratiano too would rather see his wife dead if this could save Antonio. Portia and Nerissa, standing there disguised as lawyers, have sharp comments to make on this readiness on the part of their husbands.

In the final scene Portia and Nerissa work out their joke at the expense of their husbands and Antonio, feeling guilty, now that he has been saved from death, says,

> I am the unhappy subject of their quarrels.   (V.i.279)

Finally, when Portia explains the trick they have played, and in addition produces a letter which says that three of Antonio's argosies are safely back in harbour, all Antonio can say is, "I am dumb". Portia is really too much of a know-all and contriver and this is her triumph over Antonio, to take Bassanio from him, to save his life from Shylock and to render him his argosies again. But he thanks her courteously. Portia welcomes him to her house but one feels that Antonio will be odd man out whilst he is there. Like the other Antonio he has nothing effeminate about him, and his only fault in our eyes may be his early anti-semitism. He is a dignified business man, capable of deep friendship but aware of his isolation in a heterosexual society. In this last scene Portia and Nerissa joke about infidelity in the marriage bed, but friendship is a bond which Shakespeare cannot joke about. Homosexual affection is never reciprocated in Shakespeare's plays, and it is this that makes for loneliness, but though Bassanio's instincts are unquestionably heterosexual he shows greater awareness of the depth of Antonio's love than does Sebastian of the sea captain's devotion.

I may have generalised too sweepingly, for there is the relationship between Achilles and Patroclus, where Shakespeare gives us a glimpse of a homosexual association and its unfortunate results. Achilles spends his time with Patroclus in his tent and Ulysses tries to stir him to battle, believing that the cause of Achilles' unwillingness to fight is that he is in love with a Trojan girl, Priam's daughter. But notice the words of Patroclus when Ulysses leaves.

> To this effect, Achilles, have I moved you:
> A woman impudent and mannish grown
> Is not more loathed than an effeminate man
> In time of action. I stand condemned for this;
> They think my little stomach to the war
> And your great love to me restrains you thus.
> Sweet, rouse yourself, and the weak wanton Cupid
> Shall from your neck unloose his amorous fold . . .
> (*Troilus and Cressida* III.iii.214-21)

Even then Achilles does not meet Hector fairly in combat but has him murdered by his Myrmidons. *Troilus and Cressida* is an attack on love and war, conveyed through the exposure of the Greek hero, Achilles, and the wasteful death of Hector, the fickleness of Cressida and the scurrilous contempt of Thersites for human quarrelling and lechery. The lonely ones at the end of this play are Troilus, who has lost his girl, and Andromache, who has lost her husband.

I have so far noted only possible cases of male homosexual

affection. In what most people accept as Shakespeare's part of *The Two Noble Kinsmen* there are studies of love within the confines of each of the sexes. Here again a study of the main source of the play, Chaucer's *Knight's Tale*, is revealing. Shakespeare is much indebted to Chaucer and follows his poem carefully and knowledgeably, though ruthlessly condensing for dramatic reasons. The deep bond of affection (and Chaucer uses this favourite word of Shakespeare's several times in the poem) the bond between Arcite and Palamon has no suggestion of homosexuality either in Shakespeare or in Chaucer, for when the two friends first see Emilia they each fall desperately in love with her. But the love of Theseus for Pirithous and of Emilia for Flavina are not in Chaucer. Shakespeare's addition of these two relationships to a story he otherwise followed closely must indicate an especial interest on his part. (Another addition of his, the story of the Jailer's daughter, has to do with the absurdities of heterosexual love, perhaps the main theme of the play.) The sworn, lifelong friendship between Theseus and Pirithous was a wellknown element in Greek mythology, but Flavina appears to have been Shakespeare's invention.

At the request of Theseus, Pirithous has escorted Hippolyta and Emilia to Athens. Away from his friend, he has been miserable in the company of the women and Emilia sounds Hippolyta to discover what she thinks of this.

> . . . Have you observed him,
> Since our great lord departed? (I.iii.33-4)

Hippolyta, and we remember that she has been an Amazon queen and a warrior, takes this in her stride, finding in the shared experience of the two friends enough to tie them to each other. She answers that she has observed him

> . . . With much labour;
> And I did love him for't. They too have cabined
> In many as dangerous as poor a corner,
> Peril and want contending . . . Their knot of love,
> Tied, weaved, entangled, with so true, so long
> And with a finger of so deep a cunning,
> May be outworn, never undone. I think
> Theseus cannot be umpire to himself,
> Cleaving his conscience into twain and doing
> Each side like justice, which he loves best. (I.iii.34-47)

So Hippolyta is content for the moment to leave the question open whether Theseus loves her more than Pirithous. And Emilia leaves it at that.

>   ... Doubtless
> There is a best, and Reason has no manners
> To say it is not you.   (I.iii.48-50)

Thinking along these lines she now reminds Hippolyta, for our information of course, of her own love for Flavina, who is now dead, when they were both eleven years of age. (It is significant that Palamon later gives eleven as the age when the torments of love begin, in Act V scene i line 130). Emilia gives a sensitive and beautifully phrased account of this love, a rehearsal which, she says,

>   ... has this end,
> That the true love 'tween maid and maid may be
> More than in sex dividual.   (I.iii.80-82)

Hippolyta understands that this

>   ... is but to say
> That you shall never, like the maid Flavina,
> Love any that's called man.

Emilia answers,

> I am sure I shall not.

Hippolyta finds it hard to believe that Emilia will stand by this decision, and at the same time she asserts her faith in Theseus.

> I will now in and kneel, with great assurance
> That we, more than his Pirithous, possess
> The high throne of his heart.   (I.iii.94-6)

But will Emilia be so constant in her faith? Talking about flowers with a woman in the garden, she comes upon a narcissus and they discuss the boy of that name. Emilia remarks,

> That was a fair boy, certain, but a fool
> To love himself: were there not maids enough?

She thus surely reveals a conventional attitude towards the love relationship. And when Theseus has found Palamon and Arcite fighting in the wood and in his fury threatens their death, Emily contrives to show a woman's heart by begging Theseus to spare their lives but banish them, thus making certain that they will not be able to urge protestastions of love upon her.

> . . . Swear 'em never more
> To make me their contention, or to know me,
> To tread upon thy kingdom, and to be
> Wherever they shall travel, ever strangers
> To one another.   (III.vi.253-7)

Thus she hopes to stop the silly fighting between the two friends and at the same time get rid of two embarrassing suitors. But Theseus decides that they must fight an organised duel, making a show out of their quarrel, the loser to die, the winner to have Emilia. Contemplating their portraits she feels it her duty to choose between them and stop the fight. She warms towards both of them and is horrified at the change in herself

> I am sotted,
> Utterly lost, my virgin's faith has fled me!   (IV.ii.45-6)

But she cannot choose, for the choice, of course, is being made for her by the gods, who will contrive to settle the matter by granting the prayers of the three protagonists, Arcite's to Mars for victory, Palamon's to Venus for possession of Emilia, and Emilia's prayer to Diana,

> He of the two pretenders that best loves me
> And has the truest title in't, let him
> Take off my wheaten garland, or else grant
> The file and quality I hold I may
> Continue in thy band.   (V.i.158-162)

She is Theseus' prisoner of war and cannot refuse to marry as he wishes, but she would still prefer to remain a virgin in Diana's company, for though she is already "bride-habited", ready to be given to the winner, she is still "maiden-hearted". She refuses to watch the duel but stays apart, listening to the distant shouting, and she sends a servant to find out how things are going. Arcite has won the fight, but the gaining of Emilia means the final separation from Palamon, who must now be executed. Arcite says,

> Emily,
> To buy you I have lost what's dearest to me
> Save what is bought . . . (V.iii.112-4)

But Arcite's horse throws him, he dies, Palamon is saved from execution and gets Emilia. It is Palamon who now has a similar regret to that expressed by Arcite, that though he has Emilia he has lost his friend. He speaks no word to Emilia but to Theseus, whom he

already addresses as cousin, since he is to marry the sister of Theseus'
wife,

> O cousin,
> That loss of our desire! That nought could buy
> Dear love but loss of dear love.   (V.iv.109-112)

Emilia is not given a word to speak at the end. She would have
accepted Arcite in the same silent way, as a judgement of the gods.
The persons of a drama have no life outside the play, but it is hard not
to wonder how Emilia will behave as a wife and what sort of husband
Palamon will make. We remember his mocking comments on heterosexual love in, strangely enough, his prayer to Venus.

> O thou that from eleven to ninety reign'st
> In mortal bosoms, whose chase is the world
> And we in herds thy game . . . (V.i.130-2)

He himself has so far avoided the absurdities and evils men are led
into by the power of love,

> . . . that can make
> A cripple flourish with his crutch and cure him
> Before Apollo
> . . . the polled bachelor
> Whose youth, like wanton boys through bonfires,
> Have skipped thy flame, at seventy thou canst catch
> And make him, to the scorn of his hoarse throat,
> Abuse young lays of love . . .
> . . . I knew a man
> Of eighty winters, this I told them, who
> A lass of fourteen brided. 'Twas thy power
> To put life into dust: the aged cramp
> Had screwed his square foot round,
> The gout had knit his fingers into knots,
> Torturing convulsions from his globy eyes
> Had almost drawn their spheres, that what was life
> In him seemed torture. This anatomy
> Had by his young fair fere a boy, and I
> Believe it was his . . . (V.i.85-117)

Palamon tells Venus that up till now he has steered clear of such
antics.

I have never been foul-mouthed against thy law,
Ne'er revealed secret, for I knew none . . .
        . . . I never practised
Upon man's wife, nor would the libels read
Of liberal wits; I never at great feasts
Sought to betray a beauty, but have blushed
At simp'ring sirs that did . . . (V.i.98-104)

An oddly assorted couple they are, Emilia, a high-minded lesbian, and Palamon who, up to the time of his wedding has been a type of Petrarchan lover. Theseus bids Palamon lead his lady off, but he has nothing to say to her save that he will honour Arcite. Emilia kisses Arcite before he dies, but there is no kiss for Palamon, nor a word from her to him. Shakespeare thus leaves it to us to guess how things will be between them, and to the producer of the play to decide how Emilia will look when she is led off. Here Shakespeare departs from Chaucer, who is quite sure that his Emily will make a loving wife.

For now is Palamon in alle wele,
Lyvinge in blisse, in richesse, and in hele,
And Emelye him loveth so tendrely
That never was no word hem bitwene.   (*Knight's Tale* 2101-5)

Though she has a man, and a prospective husband, to lead her off, will she be a lonely person, out of sympathy with the lavish cele-brations Theseus plans once Arcite is buried, when the men will ''put on'' ''the visages of bridegrooms'', as though that will be acting a part? It is thus possible to think of Emilia as one does of the two Antonios at the end of their plays, when wedding celebrations are toward, yet another person banished by emotional inhibitions to the periphery of normal social relationships, a bride who doesn't want to be married but has marriage thrust upon her.

I have said that, with the exception of the relationship between Achilles and Patroclus, homosexual affection is not reciprocated in the plays and poems of Shakespeare, and this accounts for the loneli-ness of Antonio the sea captain, of Antonio of Venice, of Emilia, since Flavina is dead, and possibly of Palamon, whose thoughts at the end of the play are only of Arcite. Life does not always fall into such tidy patterns as plays often end with, and Shakespeare, without over-stressing their isolation, gives us sensitive studies of persons whose emotional instincts set them apart from their fellow humans in melancholy despair.